Dec 2010

with much love

David & Pooh

Written and published by
Franck and **Jude Pontais**

www.franckpontais.co.uk

Photography
Richard Faulks

Art Direction
Mik Baines

Distribution
Navigator

First published 2008.

ISBN 978-1-903872-09-3

Terrines
&Verrines

Franck Pontais

Franck!

Franck Pontais's creations have been enjoyed by celebrities, showbusiness personalities and the Royal Family. He has dedicated his career to perfecting jaw-droppingly gorgeous, delicious food for people to share.

Born in Paris in 1972, Franck began his career at just 14. His mother, realising that schoolwork was not his forte, sent him to work as an apprentice at a butchers. After two years, with his first qualification in hand he went to Ceproc, one of the top culinary schools, where he realised he had found his true vocation. Topping his class and picking up awards for national competitions, it was here that he was baptised into the French tradition of Traiteur and learned the art of producing exquisite, gourmet food in portable portions.

Time spent in Germany on compulsory French National Service gave him a different view on catering as he cooked for 2000 soldiers. It also helped him to develop the discipline for hard work and perfectionism.

In 1996 he received a life-changing phone call offering him a job at Harrods. Aged 22 he set off immediately to London, with one suitcase and only a handful of English words, to throw himself into expanding the Traiteur counter at Harrods. Poached by Selfridges to repeat his Harrods success, he set up a Traiteur counter in both the Oxford Street and Manchester stores and helped to educate the eating habits of customers.

His next move was as a chef for London's top outside caterer. He worked for film premiers including James Bond, royal functions and for music royalty such as Elton John. He confesses that he hardly recognised many of the celebrities, coming home to wife Jude uttering cryptic descriptions such as 'the tall man that ran a hotel' for John Cleese.

In 2004 Franck and his wife Jude, who he met while working at Harrods, set up their own outside catering and events company, Food Creation. It is so successful, that people change the dates of their events in order to have Franck's creations served to their guests.

Part of the 'wow' factor in his catering comes from using verrines, a course in a glass, and innovative terrines. After years of perfecting these two versatile dishes, he now wants to convert as many cooks as possible into making these entertaining dishes a regular part of their recipe repertoire.

Franck, like all successful chefs, is positively messianic about food! 'My job is amazing. Of course the hours are long and it's hard work but it is never a chore. I have no fear of failure and so am always learning and always discovering new ways with food.'

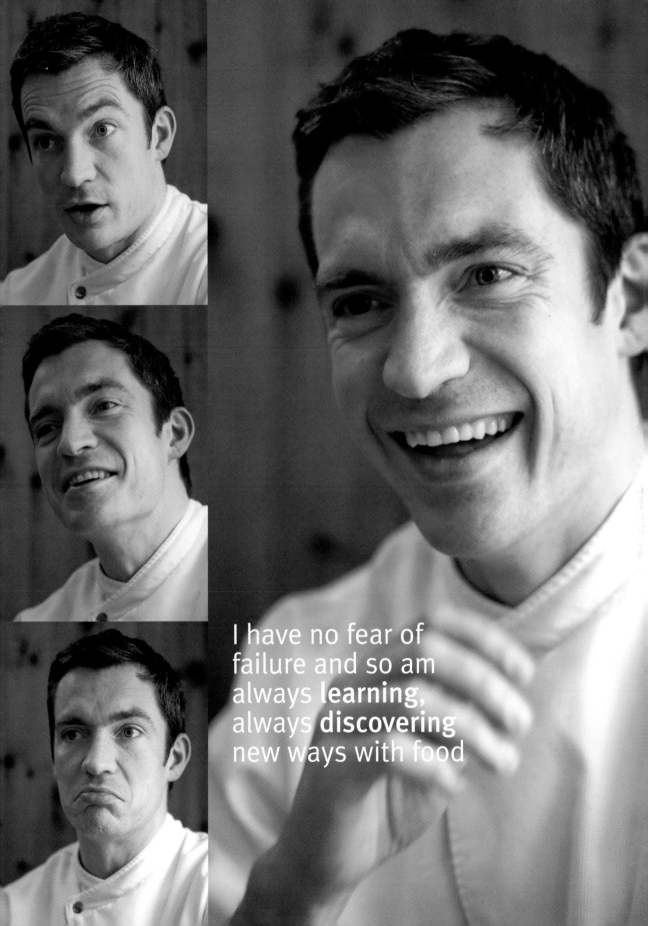

I have no fear of failure and so am always **learning**, always **discovering** new ways with food

Why a book?

Unlike most chefs who write books, Franck has never been a restaurant chef. His experience at the Traiteur counters of Harrods and Selfridges, where they sell 60 different types of terrine by the slice everyday, has given him a rare speciality.

'A terrine is really just the name for the earthenware dish it is served in rather than what's inside. I want to awaken people's imagination so that they create their own recipes. Terrines are so versatile, you don't have to make them in huge dishes for parties, they can be an everyday food. And it's a sociable dish – you make it before your guests arrive, you throw some accompaniments together, slice and serve while you chat.'

The LA Times describes verrines as 'the hottest trend you've never heard of.' They were created in France around 2001 in Michelin starred restaurants and then made their way across to LA and Las Vegas, where they were warmly embraced as a gourmet meal in a glass. A verrine is not just an opportunity to present layered food beautifully, but also to 'sink your spoon in and scoop out an explosion of flavours' says Franck. 'You have perfect portion control and you can make different kinds to appeal to all guests. Not only that, they are easily portable, people can walk around mingling with a verrine in their hand.'

Verrine is virtually an unknown term in the UK and Franck hopes to change that. Follow his step-by-step guides to producing these mini meal marvels and enjoy spreading the word.

I want to awaken people's **imagination** so that they create their own recipes... an **explosion** of flavours

Contents

See opposite for
full recipe listing

Terrines

Verrines

Getting started

Here are a few notes to help you create the best terrines and verrines using my recipes

Seasoning

I talk about this a lot, never be afraid to season well, but always remember your guests can add more if required but they cannot take it away! Always use white pepper, a cracked black pepper can leave unsightly black dots in white mixtures.

Ingredients guide

Eggs are medium and free range, cream is always double, sugar is always caster and butter is always unsalted unless stated otherwise. You can use water in place of home made stock or a stock cube. Remember that stock cubes tend to be salty.

Choosing meat & fish

Ask for advice from your butchers. They will recommend the cut of meat that you need and the maturity. A good butcher will cut or mince the meat to your requirements, saving you a job at home. Unfortunately fishmongers can be difficult to find on some high streets. Supermarkets sell a good variety of fish and the staff should be trained well to help you. When buying fish, it should be as fresh as possible, with no odour and most importantly, not slimy to the touch. I always choose a whole fish and ask for it to be filleted, this way I can see the quality of the fish.

Making the most of fresh herbs

Aromatic herbs must be kept in a damp cloth or with their stems in a little water. Parsley, chervil and chives can be chopped in advance and stored in the fridge in an air tight container. Herbs such as basil and mint should be cut and used straight away as they loose their strength, flavour and colour

A **good butcher** will cut or mince the meat to your requirements, saving you a job at home

quickly. It is important to use a very sharp knife as you want to cut the herb, and not bruise it with a blunt knife.

Dressing at the last minute
I love making and using dressings. It is vital to lightly toss the salad at the very last minute just before serving as this retains the crunchiness and freshness of the ingredients.

Cooking times can vary!
Ovens do vary, so cooking time could be affected. Remember, fan-assisted ovens tend to cook food more quickly. Using a temperature probe is very helpful. As a general rule, place it in the centre of the product – vegetables should be a minimum of 68ºC, fish 70ºC, and meat 72ºC. If the product looks cooked on top but hasn't achieved the right internal temperature then

wrap in tin foil and continue to cook. Use your own judgement, if it looks like it needs more then cook it for longer.

Working with eggs
Some of the recipes included in this book do use raw egg, particularly in the mousses. Current health advice states that pregnant women, the very young or old shouldn't eat raw egg.

Use your common sense with dish sizes
It is very difficult to anticipate the different size dishes you may use at home. I have based my terrine recipes on a 1kg loaf tin and given guides to verrine glass volumes. Each recipe tells you how many guests it will feed but if you use different sized containers then that will obviously impact on appearance.

Basil and mint should be cut and used straight away as they lose their **strength, flavour** and **colour** quickly

Terrines

What is a terrine? We see the word in cookery books and on menu cards – every great chef has at least one in their repertoire. I would however, argue that the word is not always used in it's truest form.

In essence, the word terrine refers to a china earthenware (terracotta) or cast iron cooking dish. This would be typically rectangular in shape with gently graduated sides and a tight fitting lid. Various sizes and shapes are available and the individual ones will present each guest with a whole terrine that is easily served and garnished. A china ramekin dish (covered with foil) is also useful for individual portions. Terrines with lids aid the cooking and storage. Buy a larger dish and use only part of it for smaller quantities but you will still have the larger dish for parties. A good 500g or 1kg loaf tin can be used as terrine dish if you only make them once in a while. Reduce the recipe by half for the smaller tin.

Over time, the use of the word terrine has been extended to describe the food which is cooked in the dish. The ingredients would be set, baked or pressed in this mould and turned out and sliced as a portion. So if it's been prepared in a terrine dish, is sliced and served then it is a terrine.

Being a creative chef and breaking my own rules, I went in search of other ways to present my traditional terrine. I discovered other shaped moulds to give a new dimension to the art of terrine making. Can we still technically call it a terrine? Well, I think so as it's a variation on the theme, uses the same traditional methods and achieves the same results – it's just a little different in form.

The culinary world is an artistic arena, one where the beauty of food is appreciated and I mean this in the flavours, colours and smells of all food.

Terrine making defines food as art to me – the more love, care and attention you put into the presentation the greater the rewards will be.

Remember:
Every terrine is based on producing 1kg of weight of terrine which will serve 8 guests

Pressed terrines

Pressed terrines

Pressed terrines are built using layers of ingredients and left to fuse over night with the help of weights, there's generally no need for aspic.

The time involved in creating a pressed terrine is well invested. Be a perfectionist in your ingredients preparation, cutting them to the correct thickness and depth. Most of all, take time to enjoy the layering into the mould and look forward to how eye-catching the overall effect will be.

The benefit of a pressed terrine is the merging of flavours and the union of combinations – much more subtle than in a blended mixture. Think about how the different ingredients will taste when merged and eaten together. Consider the flavours that will complement each other and of colours and textures that will give an added dimension to the terrine. Don't be afraid of strong or unusual flavour combinations, cookery is a voyage of discovery.

This method of presentation – served with a complementary sauce or crunchy biscuit – will certainly start conversations around the table.

Terrine making in this way is extremely satisfying and taking off the first slice and revealing the interior results is very exciting.

Producing a pressed terrine

Use cling film in the mould
For perfect demoulding, lightly grease the mould and lay cling film inside. Leave sufficient overhang as this will assist you in closing and pressing. Pour cold water into the lined mould as this weight will eliminate the air bubbles and creases – pour the water out and your mould is ready for use. When ready to close the terrine, pull the cling film tightly as it will be used to hold everything together. When demoulding use the cling film to ease the terrine out.

Cut the ingredients into shape
Depending on the shape and size of the mould you are using, cut the ingredients to size. You can then utilise the trimmings to fill any gaps you may have.

Seasoning
The seasoning needs to be applied between each layer as it is not possible to season the block as a whole. The best way to ensure even seasoning is to add it to your bonding mix (in most cases olive oil) and as you brush it on, it will be distributed evenly.

Build over the top
Don't stop layering the ingredients when you reach the top of the mould. Build 1 or 2 cm above the rim and when you press, this will make sure you have sufficient to fill the mould and produce a good shape and a solid result.

Preparation for pressing and the use of weights
Wrap your finished terrine in foil to protect it during the pressing process. Use a wooden board which is slightly longer and wider than your terrine. In the kitchen I use dumb bell weight ends, but never more than 2kg as it is a slow press over night, you are not looking for an instant result. At home you could use a bowl of water or a few tins of beans.

Blanching and drying
This is the action of cooking in boiling water very rapidly and cooling down in ice-cold water, it's used to fix the vibrant colour of vegetables. Blanched produce must be dried for use in a terrine to reduce the amount of water – too much moisture and the ingredients won't bond.

Storage
The pressed terrines will keep in the fridge for three to four days once wrapped in cling film, assuming you used fresh ingredients to start with. Slice only what you need. I would not suggest you freeze a pressed terrine, as when water comes into contact with the individual layers it becomes sloppy and not as formed and sturdy as it is when fresh.

 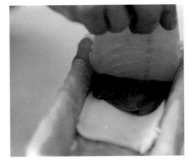 

Smoked salmon & mozzarella with basil

Method

1 Line the mould with cling film (see page 21) and lay over slices of smoked salmon.

2 Whisk the lemon juice, olive oil and seasoning to create a bonding mix.

3 Lightly brush the bonding mix onto the salmon lining. Lay the first slice of mozzarella on the bottom of the terrine mould and then top with basil leaves. Add a layer of salmon and repeat this operation until all ingredients are used and the dish is full.

4 Continue to layer the salmon and mozzarella, brushing between each layer with the bonding mix, until it reaches 1-2cm above the rim of the mould.

5 Tightly wrap and place in the fridge and apply the weights on top. The olive oil will set and become dense in the cold and will lock the layers together.

6 The following day, remove from the mould, slice and enjoy!

Advice

When buying smoked salmon, choose long sliced if you have the choice.

Serving suggestion

Serve with a shiso salad, cress and a pink peppercorn dressing (see page 192) or cut into squares and skewer for use as a canapé.

Variation

You could use different herbs such as dill or tarragon for a stronger taste.

Ingredients

500g smoked salmon, long sliced

1 lemon, juiced

100ml olive oil

Seasoning

15 leaves fresh basil

400g mozzarella block

Preparation time
30 minutes

Chilling time
12-24 hours

Serves 8

Seared tuna with avocado, new potatoes & coriander

Method

1 Line the mould with cling film (see page 21).
2 Peel the avocado and cut it into 8 wedges length ways. Set aside covered with the lemon juice to prevent browning.
3 Slice the tuna into steaks around 1 cm thick, chargrill each side for about 1 minute. Aim for the tuna to remain pink in the centre with the scorch marks on the outside, season the fish to taste.
4 Peel the new potatoes and cook in salted water until tender but firm. While still warm cut into 4 and stir into the melted butter, add the coriander.
5 Cut thin slices of aubergine lengthways, and drizzle over the olive oil. Using a hot griddle, cook the slices fully for about 30 seconds each side until translucent. Lay these into the mould on top of the cling film, leave some overhang as this will form the wrapping of the terrine.
6 Build the layers, aiming for potato, tuna, avocado, potato and a final layer of tuna. Always season between each layer and be firm when pressing in the layers, any gaps or pockets will result in an unstable terrine, which will crumble.
7 Wrap the aubergine and then cling film around to close, you may need a few extra slices of aubergine to fully cover.

Advice

Don't be afraid to use all of the lemon juice, if there is some left squeeze over the top layer of tuna before closing.

Serving suggestion

Serve with a freshly prepared moutabal, a Moroccan dip (see page 194).

Variation

Cooked sweet potato can be used in place of new potatoes.

Ingredients

1 ripe avocado

400g fresh tuna steaks

300g new potatoes

1 aubergine

1 tbsp olive oil

1 lemon, juiced

3 tbsp chopped coriander

100g unsalted butter

Seasoning

Preparation time

30 - 40 minutes

Chilling time

6 - 8 hours

Serves 8

Beef 'pot au feu' with green cabbage

Method

1 Chop turnips into 8 pieces. Cut carrots in half, lengthways. Make a slice, lengthways, through the leeks, keeping the root intact, then wash the leeks under running water. Peel and slice the shallots.

2 Cook all the vegetables in 1 litre of water with the bay leaves. Remember that there will be no further cooking so make sure the vegetables are fully cooked (without overcooking), retaining the cooking water for stock.

3 Pre-heat a griddle pan. Chargrill the steak until medium.

4 Peel leaves from the cabbage and cut in half. Blanch the cabbage and reserve the vegetable cooking water – this is now a stock.

5 Soak and squeeze the gelatine and dissolve into 500ml of the vegetable stock, this is now your bonding agent.

6 Line the mould (see page 21). Dip the cabbage into the gelatine to create a second lining for the terrine mould. Fill the mould with the vegetables and place the beef in 2 layers, after each layer add some of the stock. Wrap closed with the layer of cabbage leaves and firmly press down on the terrine to make sure it is secure.

Advice

Allow your vegetables to drain fully in the colander to get them as dry as possible – too much water and the terrine will not hold together.

Serving suggestion

Serve with a fresh horseradish mayonnaise (see page 194) and braised salsifie (see page 199).

Variation

Try using a cooked gammon, thickly sliced (1.5 – 2cm) instead of the beef.

Ingredients

100g turnips, peeled

100g carrots

150g large leeks

2 bay leaves

150g banana shallots

200g peeled new potatoes

5 gelatine leaves

250g beef, sirloin

100g green cabbage

Seasoning

Preparation time
45 minutes

Chilling time
8 - 12 hours

Serves 8

Cornfed chicken confit with mushrooms & baby leeks

Method

1 Slice the chicken into scallops. Place the chicken and the goose or duck fat with the salt in a pan, cover with tinfoil and simmer for 15 minutes.

2 Drain the chicken breast and put to one side, keeping hot. Use a little of the goose or duck fat to sauté the mushrooms with the seasoning, add the parsley and thyme at the end.

3 Blanch the baby leeks in a little salted water, cool rapidly in iced water to fix the colour. Drain and sponge off the excess water with kitchen paper.

4 Layer the mushrooms, leeks and chicken into the lined terrine dish and add a little of the fat as the bonding agent on each layer of the terrine. Remember to season as you build.

5 Place weights on top of the terrine and refrigerate overnight.

Advice

When draining and passing through the fat, keep the thyme and use it to include in the terrine as it will have absorbed some flavour. Leave a small gap between each leek to ensure the fat spreads evenly through the terrine.

Serving suggestion

Serve cold with a home made plum chutney (see page 194).

Variation

This terrine works equally well with duck breast and you should complement this with the use of duck fat. Use any mushrooms which are in season.

Ingredients

3 corn-fed chicken breasts

250g duck or goose fat

10g rock salt

100g pied de mouton mushrooms

40g chanterelle mushrooms

1 tbsp flat leafed parsley, chopped

1 tsp fresh thyme, chopped

125g baby leeks (approx 14)

Seasoning

Preparation time
40 minutes

Chilling time
6 - 8 hours

Serves 8

Artichoke, asparagus, parsnips in beetroot jus

Method

1 Line the mould with cling film (see page 21). Peel and chop the parsnip into long strips, peel and dice the beetroot. Place in a pan and cover with water to cook the parsnip with the beetroot, leave to infuse and cool for 15 minutes. Remove the parsnip, drain and blot off excess water, discard the beetroot & cooking liquid.

2 Blanch asparagus and cool in iced water.

3 Cut 6 of the artichokes into halves and the rest into 6 pieces.

4 Chop the parsley finely and add to the melted butter. Using a paint brush, brush the inside of the mould – the parsley must cover the outside of the terrine once removed.

5 Use the halved artichoke hearts as the bottom layer and season with the salt, pepper and nutmeg. Spoon over a little of the parsley butter and layer on the parsnips, then asparagus and finally the artichoke dice in the gaps.

Advice

Don't cut the root of the asparagus, snap it to determine where the tough root ends and the tender stem begins. You can get marinated artichokes from a good delicatessen. When in season use fresh artichokes.

Serving suggestion

Serve with a vanilla sauce (see page 192).

Variation

You could replace the parsnips with turnip. You could use the cooked beetroot dice inside the terrine or make a chutney.

Ingredients

250g whole parsnip

1 fresh beetroot

250g asparagus

300g globe artichokes, marinated

2 tbsp parsley, chopped

100g butter, melted

Pinch nutmeg

Seasoning

Preparation time
40 minutes

Chilling time
6 - 8 hours

Serves 8

Three peppers & feta wrapped in grilled courgette

Method

1 Cut in half and deseed the peppers, roast for 15 – 20 minutes at 220ºC, gas mark 7, in a drizzle of olive oil. Transfer to a bowl and finish the cooking by steaming covered in cling film. The steaming allows you to gently peel off the skin using the back of a teaspoon.

2 Thinly slice the courgette using a serrated knife, soak these strips in a little olive oil to prevent them burning when on the griddle. Cook the courgette on the griddle and use it to line the mould. Cut feta into slices.

For the pesto bonding agent: 3 Place the basil in a bowl and using a hand blender crush the basil (not too small) add the Parmesan and pine nuts. Add the olive oil. This should be thicker than a traditional pesto as we need it to help bond the layers.

4 Use alternate ingredients and brush with pesto sauce between each layer, fill the mould.

Advice

To make the pesto you could use a mixer in place of the hand blender.

Serving suggestion

Serve with a basil oil or make a little extra pesto.

Variation

Mozzarella works well with these strong flavours in place of the feta.

Ingredients

2 yellow peppers

2 red peppers

2 green peppers

2 courgettes sliced lengthwise

220g feta cheese

Olive oil

Seasoning

For the pesto bonding agent

4 tbsp chopped basil

2 tbsp grated Parmesan

2 tbsp pine nuts

8 tbsp olive oil

Seasoning

Preparation time
40 minutes

Cooking time
15-20 minutes

Serves 8

Fresh citrus fruits with mint in an elderflower jelly

Method

1 Peel and segment the citrus fruits. Place onto a baking tray and gently heat at 120ºC for 15 minutes to remove some of the moisture. Allow to cool.

2 Soak the gelatine in cold water, squeeze the water out and add to the cordial. Heat to a simmer to melt the leaves.

3 Peel and finely slice the mango to use as a mould lining. Arrange the base layer of citrus fruits and sprinkle over some of the biscuit crumb. Cover with cordial and lay over leaves of mint. Repeat the process until the mould is full.

Advice

Before using, soak the mint leaves in iced water to bring out a vibrant colour. Use a chop stick to penetrate into the terrine when full to make sure the jelly filters to the bottom.

Serving suggestion

Serve with spicy mango syrup (see page 193).

Variation

Use summer berries when in plentiful supply or you could use paw paw, lychee or mango for an Asian style terrine. Try using a different flavoured cordial such as ginger and lemon grass.

Ingredients

2 pink grapefruit

3 oranges

1 lemon

7 gelatine leaves

300ml water

100ml elderflower cordial

1 mango, medium sized

15 leaves mint

80g crumbed digestive biscuits

Preparation time
30 minutes

Chilling time
6 - 8 hours

Serves 8

Pudding of figs, rhubarb, strawberries & blackberries

Method
1 Reserve some nice looking berries as a garnish for the top.
2 Cut the rhubarb into 4" batons, place in a pan and pour over the orange juice. Make sure that the rhubarb is just covered. Add a little water if necessary, then sprinkle on 120g sugar. Cover with a disk of parchment paper to allow gentle steaming then cook on a low heat for 10 minutes.
3 Cut the figs and strawberries into wedges, place in a pan with the blackberries, cover with water and 60g of sugar. Simmer for 5 minutes uncovered, remove from the heat and allow to cool in their juices for a further 5 minutes.
4 Drain the fruits and reserve both liquors, mix these together in a pan and bring to the boil for 2 minutes then allow to cool.
5 To prepare the bread, remove the crusts and cut to shape, soak in the fruit syrup. Layer the dish and build in the fruits, finishing with a slice of bread on the top to close. Press firmly and drain off the excess juice which will come to the surface – don't squeeze it all out. Apply a light press over night.

Advice
Lay the terrine dish on the bread so that you can cut the strips to the exact size.

Serving suggestion
Serve with sticks of crystallised rhubarb (see page 197).

Variation
You could try crushed fresh raspberries and mint with rhubarb and serve very cold with a drizzle of lemon and golden syrup.

PRESSED **TERRINES**

Ingredients
300g sticks of rhubarb

2 oranges, juiced

180g caster sugar

300g fresh figs

225g strawberries

180g blackberries

8 slices medium white bread

Preparation time
30 minutes

Chilling time
1 hour

Serves 8

Cooked terrines

Cooked terrines

It's the cooking in this type of terrine that holds it together. Flavours merge deliciously...

This method of terrine making is probably the easiest to get you started. It's less technical and needs less precision. You can experiment more with the ingredients, flavours and textures. At the same time, don't be too adventurous, remember that some flavours simply won't harmonise together.

The style of this method of terrine making is more rustic and coarse, with more emphasis on satisfying meal solutions. I wouldn't necessarily serve these in a formal dinner party setting, more likely an informal, impromptu lunch – something I would cook for my family or have in reserve in the freezer.

These terrines are delicious enjoyed cold with chunks of fresh bread and pickles for a quick lunch. You can easily feed lots of guests in this way and as it's all created in advance, you can spend time with your guests and not your kitchen appliances!

This type of terrine doesn't necessarily need to be demoulded and sliced, you could simply spoon it out – if this is the case, remember to lightly grease the dish before filling.

Follow the step-by-step guide and you will create a great terrine that stays fresh longer than pressed terrines, as long as you keep it refrigerated.

Producing a cooked terrine

Lining the mould
Using a baking paper or parchment, line the terrine dish. Lining the dish makes it much easier to demould. If you do not wish to demould the terrine as a whole block I would recommend brushing a thin layer of butter or lard on the bottom of the dish to prevent the terrine from sticking.

Remove air bubbles
It is important to remove as much air and air bubbles from the mix as possible before cooking to improve slice presentation. To remove the bubbles, fill the terrine dish and gently knock it on the work surface, the pressure will pop the bubbles.

Enhanced flavour
For a strong flavour it is important to incorporate a good stock into your preparation. For instance, we will use a rabbit stock in the terrine (see page 45).

Pressing
You can apply a light weight during the cooling to reinforce and hold the shape.

Cooking
The cooking is critical - follow the cooking guidelines for each recipe and when you test the temperature and it's not quite done, wrap in tin foil and continue to cook. If you are creating your own terrines follow these cooking guidelines.

Meat
Cook a meat terrine at 225ºC, gas mark 7 to get some external colour and then cover with tin foil and reduce the heat to 160ºC, gas mark 3 for 40-45 minutes (based on 1kg of terrine). The terrine is cooked when interior temperature, using a probe, reads 72ºC.

Fish
A fish terrine is more delicate and needs to be cooked for longer at a lower heat. Cook for 1 hour at 150ºC, gas mark 2 for a 1kg terrine. Use a bain-marie to prevent the terrine from drying out and forming a crust. A fish terrine is cooked when the interior temperature reads 70ºC on the probe.

Storage
To prolong the storage life of the terrine you should chill it as quickly as possible. Plunge, but don't submerge, the terrine dish into a bowl of iced water for 30 minutes before storing in the fridge. Keep for up to five days wrapped in cling film in the fridge. Cooked terrines freeze well but remember, that the more water or moisture there is in the terrine to begin with, the more the structure and texture will degrade once defrosted. Defrost slowly overnight, in the fridge.

Lemon chicken breast wrapped in pork belly slices

Method

1 Slice the chicken breast into 2/3cm thick escalopes.
2 Marinate the chicken breast in the lemon syrup with fresh thyme and slices of lemon for 12 hours.
3 After lining the terrine mould (see page 41), lay raw, fine slices of pork belly into the terrine mould to form the outside crust, leave some over hanging the mould to close.
4 Mix together the minced pork belly and chicken livers, season with the salt, pepper and ginger.
5 Blanch the pistachios in boiling water for 2 minutes.
6 Build the terrine with the minced meat mix and the chicken escallops, scatter some pistachio in between each layer.
7 Fold the slices of pork belly over the top and close, pour over the marinade. Place in a bain-marie, cook at 180ºC, gas mark 4 for 1 hour.
8 Once cooked you will find the fat rises to the top of the terrine which will enable you to gently pour it out.
9 Allow to cool in the fridge for a minimum of 12 hours and slice.

Advice

If you purchase a large piece of pork belly, semi freeze it and you will get a more even slicing.

Serving suggestion

Serve with a loose hummus (see page 194).

Variation

Add whole cooked chestnuts and dried cranberries for a Christmas terrine.

Ingredients

3 large chicken breasts

120 ml lemon syrup
(see page 204)

3 slices of lemon

3 sprigs of thyme

150g pork belly, finely sliced

120g pork belly for mincing

Seasoning

100g chicken livers, whole

A pinch of ginger

50g pistachios, whole

Preparation time
40 minutes / marinate 12 hours

Cooking time
1 hour

Serves 8

43

Rabbit & pheasant marinated in mustard

Method

1 Line the mould with the pork belly slices.

2 Slice the meat into long strips, about 3cm wide.

3 Paint the mustard over the rabbit and pheasant pieces and season.

4 Sprinkle the tarragon over the meat with the cracked black pepper. Leave to marinate for at least 1 hour.

5 Poach the shallots in boiling water for 10 minutes, allow to cool and slice into long thin wedges.

6 First take the pheasant to line the mould, sprinkle over the chopped tomato and place some of the shallots in the centre. Aim to finish the terrine with the rabbit fillets and pour over the stock giving it time to soak in.

7 Cook for 1hr at 180°C, gas mark 4, in a bain-marie. When cooled, wrap with very fine slices of parma ham for a smoky flavoured finish.

Advice

Buy the rabbits pre-filleted as this is a fiddly job to do at home. To check wild produce for shot, use your fingers to gently manipulate the meat. The flavour of mustard diminishes during the cooking process therefore you can use it generously.

Serving suggestion

Serve with a mustard hollandaise (see page 193).

Variation

You could use any game for this recipe, whatever is in season.

Ingredients

200g finely sliced pork belly

3 fillets wild rabbit

4 pheasant breasts

Seasoning

100g grain mustard

1 tbsp tarragon, chopped

Pinch of cracked black pepper

1 large (or 2 small) banana shallots, peeled

2 tomatoes, diced

60ml rabbit stock

Preparation time
30 minutes

Cooking time
1 hour 10 minutes

Serves 8

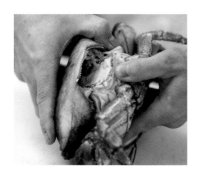

Cooked crab with celeriac & baby squid

Method

1 Skin the cod and dice, place in a blender and add seasoning, white wine and the fish stock, blitz to a paste.
2 Clean the bodies of the baby squid under fresh running water. Poach for 2 minutes in boiling water.
3 Finely slice celeriac and blanch. Line the mould with celeriac.
4 Pick out all of the white and brown meat from the crab into a bowl. Season and moisten with a little additional cooking stock.
5 Fill a piping bag with the cod paste and pipe the first layer. Between layers place the squid and the pink peppercorns. Place some sorrel leaves on top, crab and more cod paste as required.
6 Cook in the oven at 180ºC, gas mark 4 in a bain-marie for an hour and chill with a light weight on top overnight.

Advice

You can buy crab meat from a fishmonger to save you from preparing a whole crab. When sprinkling in the peppercorns, roll them in your fingers to slightly break them up.

Serving suggestion

Serve with a frozen pink peppercorn dressing (see page 192).

Variation

Could be served hot from an individual terrine, accompany with a warm hollandaise sauce.

Ingredients

350g cod fillet

Dash white wine

3 tbsp fish stock

250g baby squid

100g celeriac,
approx a quarter of a whole

250g cooked crab meat,
(approx 2 crabs weighing 450g)

Seasoning

8 leaves sorrel

1 dsp pink peppercorns

Preparation time
40 minutes

Cooking time
1 hour

Serves 8

47

Lobster, crayfish & cod with red chard

Method

1 Cook the lobsters for 8 minutes in boiling, lemon scented, water. After 7 minutes add the crayfish and simmer for a further 1.5 minutes, remove and allow to cool.

2 Season the cod and place in a blender, blitz with the double cream and 30ml of fish stock for a smooth mix.

3 Cut the lobster in half and remove the flesh.

4 Line the terrine mould with the baby spinach and at the bottom of the mould place a layer of the cod paste.

5 Place a layer of red chard leaves, the lobster meat and the chopped dill. Pour over the rest of the fish stock and add the crayfish tails.

6 Finish with the cod and close with a layer of spinach leaves.

7 Cook covered in a bain-marie for 25 minutes at 170ºC, gas mark 3.

Advice

Blanch the spinach for a few seconds before using, it makes it floppy and far easier to deal with.

Serving suggestion

Serve with an aioli emulsion (see page 193).

Variation

You could use salmon or smoked fish and serve with a spicy tomato and basil sauce.

Ingredients

350g live lobster
(around 3 lobsters
weighing 5/600g each)

1/2 lemon

100g crayfish

Seasoning

350g diced cod

40ml double cream

60ml fish stock

150g spinach

20g red chard leaves

1 sprig fresh chopped dill

Preparation time
30 minutes

Cooking time
25 minutes

Serves 8

49

Two rice with broccoli & cauliflower

Method

1 Blanch the cauliflower and broccoli florets in vegetable stock, keep the stock for later use.

2 Cook rice in 300ml of milk with turmeric. When cooked, season to taste.

3 Arrange hot rice with interspersed vegetables in your chosen terrine.

4 Pour 250ml of stock over the rice to keep the terrine moist while cooking.

5 Cook in a bain-marie at 190°C, gas mark 5 for 30 minutes, leave to cool and set in the fridge. To keep it moist slice only when ready to serve.

Advice

You do not need to fully cook the rice as it will finish cooking in the terrine – over cooking will result in a sloppy, unstable terrine. I would apply a light weight during cooling to hold the shape.

Serving suggestion

Serve with pickled vegetables (see page 198) and large caperberries or a strong mustard.

Variation

Add lots of chopped coriander and sultanas for a Moroccan twist and serve with a yoghurt dressing.

Ingredients

250g cauliflower

220g broccoli (approx 1 head)

1 litre vegetable stock

100g wild rice

125g basmati rice

300ml milk

1 tsp turmeric

Seasoning

Preparation time
30 minutes

Cooking time
30 minutes

Serves 8

Wild mushrooms & garlic baked with roasted turnip

Method

1 Peel and cut the turnips into wedges. Crush the garlic to release the aroma, you need not remove the skin. Place the diced turnip and garlic in a roasting tray with the olive oil, bay leaves and thyme, sprinkle over the rock salt. Roast for 15 minutes at 200⁰C, gas mark 6.

2 Remove the garlic from the tray and gently press each clove to release from the skin. Puree into a paste, add to a frying pan with the butter. Add the wild mushrooms and gently sauté until cooked then add the turnips.

3 Finely chop half of the rocket and add to the beaten egg, the cream and the breadcrumbs.

4 Place a spoonful of the rocket mixture at the bottom of the mould, place in some mushrooms and turnips and then the rocket mix, keep layering until full. Aim to finish the dish with a layer of mushrooms and turnips. Bake for 15 minutes at 200⁰C, gas mark 6.

Advice

Leave the mushrooms in large pieces as this is a rustic terrine. This terrine is better presented in individual serving pots as the fragrance when you delve in is divine.

Serving suggestion

This is so fragrant and tasty, simply serve with an undressed rocket leaf salad.

Variation

This dish is excellent for vegetarians. You could also add a drizzle of hazelnut oil.

Ingredients

500g turnips

1 garlic bulb

50ml olive oil

2 bay leaves

1 tbsp chopped thyme

Sprinkle rock salt

30g butter

350g assorted mushrooms

100g rocket

3 eggs beaten

60ml double cream

3 tbsp breadcrumbs

Preparation time
20 minutes

Cooking time
30 minutes

Serves 8

Dark chocolate & orange

Method

For the orangette: **1** Melt the chocolate in a bain-marie
2 Peel the orange, take the rind, cut into long strips and blanch them twice (blanch once, replace the water and repeat).
3 Bring the water and sugar to the boil, add the orange peel and simmer for 5 minutes, leave to cool.
4 Drain off the syrup and dip into the melted chocolate. Allow to set on parchment paper.

For the terrine: **1** Bring the cream to a gentle simmer in a saucepan.
2 Mix the cornflour and cocoa powder together and whisk into the cream, remove from the heat. Keep whisking until dissolved, transfer into a mixing bowl.
3 Whisk the eggs and muscovado sugar together until foamy then add the Cointreau.
4 Mix into the hot mixture and combine. Finally, add the remaining melted chocolate from the orangettes.
5 Pour the mix into a lined terrine mould and layer in the orangettes.
6 Cover with a lid or tin foil. Cook in a bain-marie at 200ºC, gas mark 6 for 1 hour, removing the lid after 45 minutes. Cook for a further 15 minutes. Chill for 6 to 8 hours with the lid off.

Advice

Use a long thin terrine dish for optimum cooking efficiency.

Serving suggestion

Serve with a hot chocolate sauce (see page 193), and/or a mango syrup (see page 193).

Variation

You can substitute coffee for the orange flavour. Dissolve a teaspoon of instant coffee granules in a small amount of hot water and add to the mix before pouring into the mould.

Ingredients

200g dark chocolate

1 orange

100ml water

50g sugar

250 ml double cream

40g corn flour

40g cocoa powder

4 eggs

2 tbsp muscovado sugar

2 tbsp Cointreau

Preparation time
30 minutes

Cooking time
1 hour

Chilling time
6-8 hours

Serves 8

Coconut semolina with dried fruit

Method

1 Line the dish with baking parchment. Brush with melted butter.
2 Soak the sultanas in the rum, soak the apricots in the coconut milk, each for a minimum of 6 hours. Drain and reserve the milk and all of the rum should have been absorbed.
3 In a pan, heat the coconut milk and semi skimmed milk. Remove the seeds from the vanilla pod and add to the mixture with the pod. When simmering, add the semolina, keep stirring for a minute and remove from the heat.
4 Slowly whisk the eggs with the sugar and vanilla essence, add to the semolina, then add the fruit.
5 Pour into the mould and sprinkle a few more sultanas on top. Cook in a bain-marie for 30 minutes at 200°C, gas mark 6.

Advice

Brush the surface with melted butter to prevent a crust forming.

Serving suggestion

Serve warm with a hot dark rum sauce (see page 193).

Variation

In place of the semolina you could use pudding rice, the flavours work well and it creates a different texture.

Ingredients

5g melted butter

50g sultanas

2 tbsp rum

80g dried apricots

300ml semi skimmed milk

300ml coconut milk

1 vanilla pod

140g dried semolina

2 eggs

40g sugar

1 tbsp vanilla essence

80g prunes, de-stoned

Preparation time
20 minutes

Cooking time
45 minutes

Chilling time
Minimum 2 hours

Serves 8

Set terrines

59

Set terrines

This type of terrine won't need to be cooked as it sets using natural ingredients or gelling agents. It can be prepared well in advance and sliced just before you serve.

The main difference between set and pressed terrine is that it binds together and because you don't need to use weights, you can include some more delicate ingredients. If you produce a terrine which is higher than the terrine mould, you could use a light weight to reinforce the shape. Fish is naturally gelatinous, however, when working with other ingredients you may need to use bonding agents such as butter or gelatine.

Judicious seasoning and respect for the raw materials will give you a great result. Be aware that if the ingredients contain too much water, this moisture will slowly release and make the terrine impossible to slice. Be especially careful with fruits like citrus or tomatoes.

The beauty of this terrine technique is the use of stock and glaze or the liquid retained from cooking vegetables. The set terrine is a remarkable way to mix flavours – use the gel as a background overall flavour and highlight with overtones which work with each other but also in harmony with the gel. The trick with these terrines is to get just the right amount of gelatine in the gel – too much and it will result in a rubbery consistency, too little and it will not hold and produce a clean slice.

Working with gelatine is explained a little further in the technical info section (see page 200).

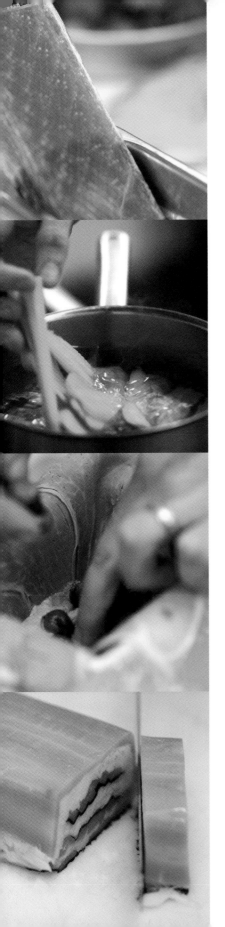

Producing a set terrine

Preparing the mould
I would not suggest you line the entire mould as this could affect the outside look of the terrine once out of the mould. Instead use a strip of baking parchment and lay it length ways on the base of the mould, leave some overhang which you can use to pull the terrine from the mould.

Prepping the ingredients
Cook the raw ingredients in a jus or stock and allow the flavours to infuse in the stock for around 30 minutes before draining. Once you have removed the ingredients from this liquid you should reduce it slowly by a third to intensify the flavours. Taste the liquid and season if necessary.

Bonding
In some cases you will need to use an additional bonding ingredient such as butter, goose fat or olive oil. However, in some recipes the ingredients themselves will generate the gel – fish and meat bones are a good example.

Texture & form
It is vital to dry the vegetables and other moist ingredients, as too much moisture will prevent the terrine setting and it will fall apart when sliced. When cooking vegetables they should be just cooked, over-cooking will result in a mushy terrine. Do remember that under-cooked vegetables will be very noticeable as the terrine as a whole will have no further cooking.

In the mould
Take your time arranging the ingredients. The more effort you make, the greater the satisfaction with your attractive final terrine.

Chilling
I like to make set terrines the day before I need them, allowing them to set slowly overnight. The consequences of impatience with this type of terrine are severe. Demould too soon and you will be punished with a sloppy puddle instead of a heavenly slice.

Demoulding
Place the dish upside down on a cooling rack and pass the bottom under a stream of warm (not hot) water. This action melts the bottom of the terrine and with a gentle pull on the greaseproof paper, it should easily pop out of the mould.

Slicing
I would recommend putting the terrine block back in the fridge for a further 30 minutes after demoulding to allow the softened terrine bottom to reset.

Skate with gherkins, carrots & sushi nori

Method

1 Finely slice the carrots lengthways and blanch in fish stock.
2 Line an ovenproof tray with paper and add the skate, juniper berries, star anise and lemon cut into wedges. Cover with fish stock and sprinkle over the rock salt and dill. Poach at 220°C, gas mark 6 for 15 minutes.
3 Dice the gherkins.
4 While the fish is still warm, gently remove the flesh using the back of a spoon.
5 Line the mould with the blanched carrot strips. Layer the ingredients into the terrine dish, in the centre place a layer of the sushi nori, ending with the carrots.
6 Allow to set for a minimum of 4 hours, I recommend making this terrine the day before and allowing to set overnight.

Advice

Don't be afraid to add a few spoons of fish stock when building the terrine, skate is very rich in natural gelatine and will set.

Serving suggestion

Serve with fried capers and a tomato & lemon concasse (see page 199).

Variation

You could use sushi nori to line the terrine mould and use the carrots inside the terrine, this would give a different view on presentation.

SET **TERRINES**

Ingredients

200g carrots

1 litre fish stock

800g skate wing (approx 2)

3 juniper berries

2 star anise

Fresh lemon

Sprinkle rock salt

1 tsp dill

60g gherkins

2 sushi nori

Preparation time
15 minutes

Cooking time
15 minutes

Chilling time
4-6 hours

Serves 8

Smoked mackerel & trout with saffron potatoes

Method

1 Boil the potatoes with saffron strands until soft and thoroughly cooked, drain and keep hot.

2 Line the mould using the cooked mackerel fillets.

3 Add to the slightly cooled potatoes, chopped dill, melted butter and seasoning. Using your hands, crush the potatoes and press firmly into the mould.

4 Just before you reach half way up the terrine, place in the smoked trout fillets, add more potatoes and finish with the mackerel.

Advice

Build this terrine while the potatoes are still warm as it is the action of the starch and the butter cooling together that binds the terrine.

Serving suggestion

Serve with a crisp green salad and chilled white wine.

Variation

Any smoked fish fillets will work well in this terrine such as haddock or smoked eel.

Ingredients

300g new potatoes, peeled

pinch saffron

400g fillets of smoked mackerel, skin on

1 tsp fresh dill, chopped

100g melted butter

200g fillets of smoked trout

Seasoning

Preparation time
30 minutes

Chilling time
4-6 hours

Serves 8

Ham & pork liver mousse with cherries & baby onions

Method

1 Line the terrine with fine slices of ham.

2 Make a caramel with the sugar and olive oil and then add the cherries and onions, gently heat until covered in caramel. Add the port and further toss the cherries and onions, remove from the heat and reserve.

3 Soak the gelatine leaves and squeeze out excess water, melt into the boiling vegetable stock.

4 In a blender combine the pork liver mousse with the melted butter, then put in a piping bag and pipe the bottom layer of the mould. Put a slice of ham on top of this and then sprinkle in some of the cherries and onions, cover with a ladle of vegetable stock. Pipe another layer of mousse mix and continue until all ingredients are used and the dish is full.

Advice

You can buy pork mousse at a good deli or supermarket. When fresh cherries are not in season (or really expensive) you can use tinned cherries which are already pitted.

Serving suggestion

Serve with thin, crisp panatonne Melba toasts (see page 195) as a great contrast to the smooth mousse.

Variation

You could use duck mousse instead of pork.

Ingredients

30g sugar / 2 tbsp olive oil for caramel

100g pitted cherries

100g baby silverskin onions

3 tsp port

3 gelatine leaves

200g pork liver mousse

50g butter, melted

250g smoked ham, finely sliced

150ml vegetable stock

Preparation time
30 minutes

Chilling time
Overnight

Serves 8

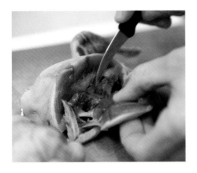  

Duck magret & quail breast confit cooked with apple

Method

1 Remove the breast from the quail (your butcher could do this).
2 Peel apples and cut into wedges.
3 Trim the duck and score the skin. Using the palm of your hand, rub the rock salt on the flesh side and shake off the excess.
4 Season the quail.
5 Preheat the frying pan with 1 tbsp of the goose fat.
6 Fry the duck breast, skin side down, until golden and crisp. Transfer to a baking tray in the oven to finish for about 10 minutes at 220°C, gas mark 7. Allow to rest for 15 minutes.
7 In the same fat, fry the quail breast skin side down for 3 to 5 minutes and sprinkle with cumin seeds.
8 Deglaze the pan with a splash of port and put the quail to one side. Add the apple wedges and a sprinkling of cumin. Add in the apple jelly, cook for 5 minutes and remove from heat.
9 Slice the duck breast to create thick scallops.
10 Line the terrine mould with cling film and place the meat around the outside, into the gaps press in the apple, place in more meat and repeat.

Advice

Firmly press down on the terrine to make sure a good shape and wrap well with cling film so that you don't lose any juices.

Serving suggestion

Serve with crisp apple wedges.

Variation

This recipe would work well with ripe plums instead of the apple.

Ingredients

8 quail breasts

3 Granny Smith apples

180g apple jelly
(see page 206)

1 duck breast

50g rock salt

Seasoning

2 dsp goose fat

1 tbsp port

Sprinkle cumin seeds

Preparation time
40 minutes

Cooking time
15 minutes

Chilling time
4 hours with light weight

Serves 8

Sweet potato & celery with dill cream cheese

Method

1 Prepare the vegetables by trimming and cutting to the size of the terrine mould you are using.
2 Blanch the celery in salted water, drain and chill in iced water. Drain and dry with kitchen paper. Repeat with the sweet potato.
3 Soak and squeeze the gelatine leaves.
4 Heat the cream cheese until melted, add the gelatine leaves and then the mustard, chopped dill and seasoning.
5 Place half of the vegetables into the mould in a checker board design and pour over half of the hot cream cheese. Tap on the table to remove the air bubbles and fill with the remaining vegetables and cream cheese. Allow to set overnight.

Advice

The celery, by nature, is U shaped. When putting into the mould place it with the dip facing up to allow the mixture to fill the gaps.

Serving suggestion

Serve with a homemade tomato jam (see page 194).

Variation

You could flavour and colour the cream cheese further by adding some tomato puree or chopped spinach.

Ingredients

325g sweet potato

325g celery

4 gelatine leaves

350g cream cheese

1 tbsp chopped dill

1 tsp grain mustard

Seasoning

Preparation time
20 minutes

Chilling time
Overnight

Serves 8

Old fashioned Macedoine presented as a mosaic

Method

1 Cut all of the vegetables to a mirepoix (see page 201) and blanch in vegetable stock. Do not over cook, the vegetables should be al dente, as a guide use a knife and gently spear the pieces to test.
2 Drain the vegetables and reserve the stock.
3 Soak the gelatine leaves and squeeze out the water, then add to the hot vegetable stock.
4 Put all vegetables into a bowl, season well, add the chopped parsley. Pour over the stock and leave to set.

Advice

Make sure the vegetables are well drained, the less water content you have the better the result for this terrine.

Serving suggestion

Serve with a pink mustard mayonnaise (see page 195).

Variation

This dish is similar to a Macedoine better known as 'Russian Salad' in England. You could add a dash of vodka into the stock and serve with cold mayonnaise to make it more authentic.

Ingredients

150g carrots

150g french beans

150g peas

150g parsnip

300ml vegetable stock

4 gelatine leaf

1 tsp parsley, flat leaf chopped

Seasoning

Preparation time
25 minutes

Chilling time
1 hour until firm

Serves 8

Mango, papaya, fresh berries & dates

Method
1 Peel the fruit and deseed the papaya.
2 Line the terrine mould with cling film (see page21). Cut fine slices of mango and line the mould.
3 Cut the papaya in half and divide each half into 8 strips.
4 Deseed the dates.
5 Layer all ingredients into the mould.
6 Soak and squeeze the gelatine leaves. Dilute the cordial into the water over a gentle heat. Dissolve the gelatine leaves in the liquid, making sure they dissolve completely.
7 Allow to cool slightly and pour this mixture over the fruits. The liquid must filter through the fruit.

Advice
Gently knock the terrine on the table to ensure the cordial mixture goes all the way through.

Serving suggestion
Serve with a mint and passion fruit dressing (see page 192).

Variation
This terrine would also work very well using different varieties of melon cut into wedges.

Ingredients

1 large mango

1 papaya

8 dried dates

125g strawberries

125g raspberries

350ml water

100ml ginger cordial

5 gelatine leaves

Preparation time
30 minutes

Chilling time
4 hours

Serves 8

Vanilla panacotta with cherries, plums & sultanas

Method

1 Soak the gelatine in the milk and squeeze.
2 Whisk together the milk, cream, sugar and vanilla essence, then bring to a simmer.
3 Add the gelatine, whisk well until dissolved. Once well mixed, remove from the heat and pass through a sieve.
4 Pour quarter of the liquid into the mould and add about a third of the fruit. Allow to set in the fridge for about 15 minutes. Repeat this until all ingredients are used up.

Advice

Allow each layer to set before adding more fruit or everything will sink to the bottom with no even spread throughout the terrine. Use different fruit in each layer.

Serving suggestion

Serve with balsamic cherry griottine dressing (see page 192) and eat at room temperature.

Variation

Not all guests will enjoy the alcohol taste of the cherry griottine. You could use some tinned cherries, but do make sure they are well drained before adding to the terrine.

Ingredients

5 gelatine leaves

200ml semi skimmed milk

400ml double cream

100g caster sugar

1 tbsp vanilla essence

100g dried mirabelle plums

100g dried red plums

40g golden sultanas

50g cherry griottine

Preparation time
15 minutes

Chilling time
4 hours

Serves 8

Eggs & cream terrines

Eggs & cream

Eggs, cream and bread are all great as bonding elements. They also bring moisture and softness into the terrine and are particularly useful with strong flavours of game or fish. They produce a light and airy texture, as well as a very soft even texture to the palate.

We could almost compare some recipes to making a simple loaf or a cake where the baking tin is replaced with a terrine mould. We employ the same cooking technique as the cooked terrine and it is not unusual to press this kind of terrine when cooling down to fix a good, structured shape which will produce a tidy slice. Aside from flavour, using dairy as a terrine base allows one to slice thinly and to serve it in different ways. Because it is easy to slice you could even use it as a topping for crisp crostinis as a canapé or starter.

An attractive terrine is achieved if you consider it like a gratin or a lasagne. Once cooked you can reheat in the oven and serve warm. I would always chill the terrine first to demould and then thoroughly reheat when ready to serve, of course, you could cook and then serve immediately to eliminate the reheating or serve cold.

You can substitute cream for a denser, more savoury crème fraîche which will give a smoother result.

Producing eggs and cream terrines

Lining the mould
Line the terrine with parchment paper if you intend to demould the terrine and serve it cold. Spread a little fat such as butter or lard on the inside of the mould if you prefer to serve it hot, directly from the dish.

Seasoning and marinating for meat terrines
You will need to marinate and season any meat at least a few hours before using it in the terrine. Finely mince the meat, if you don't have a grinder or a food processor at home you could ask your butcher to do it. Always season it after grinding.

Flavour
It is better to use free range eggs as I believe you end up with a better tasting terrine.

Quantities
As a general guide use 2 eggs per kg of minced meat with 150g of double cream. Use 4 eggs per kg of fish with 300g of double cream (half the cream quantity if using crème fraîche). I add 100g of fresh bread crumbs to fish terrines for a better texture.

In the oven
Always cook these terrines in a bain-marie to prevent them from drying out. Cook covered with a lid or in tin foil to avoid giving colour to the crust. It is essential that the core of the terrine reaches 72°C for meat and 70°C for fish.

Chilling
Chill quickly in a basin full of ice for 30 minutes before transferring to the fridge for storage. I would chill the whole loaf for at least 12 hours before slicing.

Chicken, mozzarella & red onion compote

Method

For the compote: Chop the onion into fine slices, add the wine, sugar and water to a pan. Sweat down for 30 minutes on a low heat, mixing with a wooden spoon from time to time.

For the terrine: **1** Dice the chicken breast and mince half of it, leaving the other half as a dice.
2 Marinate the chicken in the white wine, seasoning and nutmeg, for at least 1 hour.
3 Dice the mozzarella into cubes the same size as the chicken dice.
4 Add the cream and egg to the chicken, then add the mozzarella and mix well.
5 Add a layer of the chicken to the terrine mould and then some onion compote, continue to fill the terrine, you are aiming for the onion to be marbled throughout the terrine.
6 Cook covered for 25 minutes at 180°C, gas mark 4.

Advice

You can make the onion compote ahead of time and store it in the fridge. This compote works well with other meats or strong cheddar cheese.

Serving suggestion

Serve with fried basil leaves (see page 198).

Variation

This terrine is also very tasty with a caramelised shallot compote, but you would need to balance this sweetness with a sharp sherry dressing.

Ingredients

For compote

1 red onion

100ml red wine

50g Demerara sugar

100ml water

Terrine

2 medium chicken breasts

1 tbsp dry white wine

Seasoning and nutmeg

250g mozzarella

80ml double cream

2 eggs

170g red onion compote (see above)

Preparation time
20 minutes
1 hour marinating

Cooking time
30 minutes for compote
25 minutes for terrine

Serves 4

Spinach, ricotta & pancetta with grilled red peppers

Method

1 Dice the pancetta and sear until golden in a non-stick frying pan.
2 Sauté the spinach in the pancetta fat. Squeeze the spinach in a sieve with the back of a wooden spoon and dice roughly. Mix in a bowl with ricotta, cream, eggs and seasoning.
3 Deseed the peppers and cut in half, brush with olive oil. Roast in the oven at 200ºC, gas mark 6 for 15 minutes. Remove from the oven and transfer to a bowl and cover with cling film. Allow to rest, when cool, remove the skin of the peppers using the back of a teaspoon.
4 Using a very hot griddle, chargrill the peppers to give a charred taste. Line the mould with the red peppers.
5 Pour the mixture into the lined mould and cook in a bain-marie for 40 minutes at 200ºC, gas mark 6.

Advice

You can buy marinated red peppers in jars.

Serving suggestion

Serve with wild rocket.

Variation

If you can't find smoked pancetta use your favourite cooked meat, such as smoked chicken, ham or turkey.

Ingredients

200g smoked pancetta piece

250g baby leaf spinach, washed and drained

200g ricotta cheese

40ml double cream

Seasoning

2 eggs

4 red peppers

Preparation time
15 minutes

Cooking time
55 minutes

Chilling time
2 hours

Serves 8

85

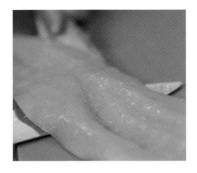

Smoked haddock mousse with herbs & cambozola

Method

1 Remove the skin from the haddock and cut 200g of it into scallops. Also slice all the cod into scallops.
2 Blend the remaining smoked haddock with the cream and a squeeze of lemon juice then season. Finish by adding the eggs and mix together making a mousse.
3 Line the mould with the haddock scallops, place the more yellow side facing out for better appearance.
4 Lay the scallops of cod and spoon over the mousse. Layer on some chunks of the cheese and then add more mix. In between layers sprinkle with fresh herbs.
5 Cook for 20 minutes at 200ºC, gas mark 6 in a bain-marie.

Advice

Let this terrine cool down completely before you try to slice it. Use a serrated knife and saw across the terrine – don't push down on it and squash it.

Serving suggestion

Serve with sweet caramelised peaches.

Variation

The cambozola in this terrine is very runny (but provides an excellent flavour). If you prefer something that holds together a little better, try a Roquefort or Stilton but use a bit less.

Ingredients

400g smoked haddock

300g cod

50ml cream

Squeeze of lemon juice

2 eggs

150g cambozola chunks

Seasoning

1 tbsp flat leaf parsley, chopped

1 sprig thyme or half a tsp of dried

Preparation time
35 minutes

Cooking time
20 minutes

Chilling time
2 hours

Serves 8

87

Salmon, cod & prawn mousse with lemon & fennel

Method

1 Remove the fish skin, trim and make sure there are no bones.
2 Dice the fennel and sweat gently in a pan with the butter
3 Blitz two thirds of each fish separately in the blender, reserving one third to dice or leave whole for instance, the prawns. Season each of the mixes and add a dash of white wine.
4 Mix the eggs with the cream, divide equally between each fish and mix. To each of these add some of the diced fish which you should consider by colour, for instance add prawn into the cod, salmon into the prawn and cod into the salmon.
5 Add the cooked fennel into each, mix well and season.
6 Take a spoon and randomly fill the lined terrine dish, again being aware of the colours you are spooning. Aim for a rustic look.
7 Cook, covered in foil, in a bain-marie for 35 minutes at 200ºC, gas mark 6. Allow to cool with a light weight placed on top to ensure stability and shape.

Advice

Make sure your fish is very fresh, as fish ages its texture changes. Try to work with cold equipment, so keep your mixing bowl in the freezer.

Serving suggestion

Served with fennel and cumin confit in butter and lemon juice (see page 199).

Variation

Using mussel, crayfish or cockles will give the terrine more texture.

Ingredients

250g salmon fillet, fresh

2 bulbs of fennel

20g butter

250g cod

250g freshwater prawns, cooked

30ml dry white wine

2 eggs

150ml double cream

Seasoning

Preparation time
40 minutes

Cooking time
35 minutes

Serves 8

89

Caramelised onions, ham & reblochon cheese

Method

1 Very slowly sweat the onions in the butter, you are aiming for them to soften without taking on too much colour.
2 Cook the potatoes thoroughly in boiling water. Slice the reblochon.
3 Break the eggs and season, whisk well with the double cream, a splash of white wine and nutmeg.
4 Slice the potatoes into escalopes (not too thin) to approximately the same thickness as the cheese.
5 Build the ingredients into the lined mould, finishing with the cream mix ensuring it filters throughout the terrine. Finish with a slice of cheese on top.
6 Cook at 200°C, gas mark 6 for 20 minutes.

Advice

If you plan to make these in individual terrines and serve them directly to your guests you could finish cooking under the grill and serve bubbling and golden.

Serving suggestion

Serve with hot biscotte (see page 195).

Variation

You could use a different French cheese such as Port Salut which is more widely available.

Ingredients

4 white onions, finely sliced

30g butter

200g new potatoes, peeled

300g reblochon cheese

2 eggs

80ml double cream

2 tbsp white wine

Pinch nutmeg

200g smoked ham, diced

Seasoning

Preparation time
30 minutes

Cooking time
20 minutes

Serves 8

Goats cheese, rocket & baby onions with chorizo

Method

1 Line the mould with baking paper. Finely slice the chorizo and use to line the mould, reserve the rest to close.
2 Blend the cornflour into half the cream (it will be rather thick). Add 2 eggs and whisk well.
3 Remove the outside 'skin' of the goats cheese and heat with the remaining cream until almost melted.
4 In the terrine dish layer in the rocket, the sundried tomatoes and onions.
5 Cover with the cream mix and bang on the table to eliminate air bubbles. Finish with a layer of chorizo.
6 Cook at 200°C, gas mark 6 for 35 minutes covered with tin foil.

Advice

A good deli will slice the chorizo for you, it is a little difficult to get very thin by hand. You can use sliced, sweated onions in place of the baby ones if you wish.

Serving suggestion

Serve with fine slices of deep fried chorizo served cold and crisp and use the dressing from the tomatoes drizzled over.

Variation

You could caramelise the baby onions in a little olive oil and sugar to bring a little more sweetness to the dish.

Ingredients

120g chorizo sausage

15g cornflour

50ml double cream

3 eggs

150g goats cheese

2 tbsp fresh rocket, chopped

120g sundried tomatoes

50g baby onions, cooked

Preparation time
20 minutes

Cooking time
35 minutes

Serves 8

93

Frozen dried fruits & nuts in nougatine parfait

Method

1 Make a clear caramel with water and sugar, remove at 110°C.
2 Using a food mixer, whisk egg yolks until foamy and then pour the caramel slowly on top (this action cooks the eggs), continue to whisk until cool.
3 Whisk the double cream by hand, until firm and add to the mix.
4 Roughly chop the fruit and nuts and mix well into the cream and egg mixture.
5 Fold gently as you do not want to remove the air that you have generated. Pour into a lined terrine mould, tap gently on the table to eliminate the air bubbles and freeze over night.

Advice

As this is frozen I always make a large batch of it to keep in reserve. Allow a little longer to set if you are using a shallow terrine.

Serving suggestion

Serve with home made cherry biscotti (see page 195).

Variation

You could adapt this recipe for many flavours for instance rum and sultana or honey and cranberry.

Ingredients

180g sugar

100ml water

8 egg yolks

200ml double cream

70g mixed peel

70g french glacé cherries

70g dried apricots

35g pistachio nuts

80g flaked almonds

Preparation time
25 minutes

Chilling time
Freeze overnight

Serves 8

Mango & chocolate polenta

Method

1 Dissolve the cocoa powder in 50ml of milk in the microwave.
2 Bring the remaining milk to a simmer with the cream and sugar. Add the polenta on a low heat and cook for 5 to 8 minutes, continually stirring with a wooden spoon.
3 Add the egg in the last minutes of cooking and divide the mix into 2 bowls. Pour the mango into one and the chocolate milk into the other.
4 Spoon both into a lined terrine mould making a nice pattern.
5 Cover and chill.

Advice

Be quick when pouring the mix into the terrine, it does set quite fast.

Serving suggestion

Serve with a hot chocolate sauce and Crème Anglaise (see page 193).

Variation

When experimenting with flavour combinations on this one do consider the colour contrast, try strawberry and vanilla for instance.

Ingredients

2 tbsp cocoa powder

550ml milk

80g sugar

90g double cream

180g dried polenta

1 egg

4 tbsp mango puree

Preparation time
15 minutes

Chilling time
2 hours

Serves 8

Making the most of terrines

As a chef who has been involved in banqueting and outside catering for much of my career, I know the importance of being ready when guests arrive and only having to put the finishing touches on at the last minute.

Terrines are great for entertaining as most of the hard work is done in advance. With a little fresh last minute garnish or accompaniment you can serve a beautiful starter totally relaxed, with all the preparation behind you. Terrines should be moist and fresh so don't slice too far in advance.

Dinner parties
Slice the terrine and present on individual plates. You could try putting a whole terrine down and slicing it for guests at the table. Or you could pre-slice it and present on a platter for guests to serve themselves. Garnish the tray with salad leaves and chutney or sauce.

Buffet
Whole blocks of terrine work very well on a buffet. They allow a meat, fish and vegetable variation on a theme (I hate it when vegetarians are offered something second rate as an after thought when there are so many great ingredients to be used). Do ensure the terrines that you offer are well formed and >>

Lemon chicken
breast wrapped
in pork belly
slices.
Page 43

Making the most of terrines

stable, once your guests have been helping themselves things can get a little messy. Serve with bowls of accompaniments and whole loaves of bread.

Drinks reception or canapés

You can use little forks or wooden skewers to present one bite sized portion of terrine – pressed ones particularly lend themselves to this method of presentation. For people to enjoy the best mouthful on a stick, cut little disks of bread to skewer with the terrine portion. When creating canapés I always think of ladies in their best dresses – don't make them too large or fragile, a spillage is embarrassing for everyone!

Picnic or packed lunch

Terrines will hold together well and for a picnic, I would slice a whole block into portions and then put them together again to keep each piece fresh as possible. Do be careful to keep the terrine cold, some will lose structural integrity if they get a little warm.

For the freezer

If you pack them well, terrines will freeze and defrost well (with the exception of a set terrine). I would recommend making more terrine than you need and storing it for a great mid-week treat or for when unexpected guests turn up. I recommend defrosting slowly in the fridge over night if possible.

Smoked
salmon and
mozzarella
with basil.
Page 23

When creating canapés I always think of ladies in their best dresses – don't make them too large or fragile, a spillage is embarrassing for everyone!

Seared tuna
with avocado,
new potatoes
& coriander.
Page 25

Verrines

A verrine is a beautiful, self-contained masterpiece that gives you the opportunity to experiment with flavours, textures and presentation. The word verrine comes from *verre*, the French for a glass dish.

It is a simple concept: layered food, typically served as a starter or dessert presented in a glass, but it could also be a main course. However, you can't serve a verrine in any old glass – particularly if it is cooked in the oven. Choose glasses to your own taste but care must be taken if you are preparing cooked verrines to use only ovenproof glass without a stem. Small preserving jars can be used. You will see in the pictures, some shot glasses and tumblers filled with verrine recipes. Do check to see if a spoon or fork will reach the bottom of the verrine to make sure that your guests can eat all the contents.

When you invent your own verrines, consider how the layers will harmonise and textures will compliment. A verrine can have many layers, my best advice is to aim for odd numbers, as I find it's easier on the eye. Consider how they will all taste as your guest digs the spoon into the layers and scoops out a mouthful filled with different sensations.

The history of verrines is a short story. Invented in Michelin-starred restaurants around seven years ago they have become commonplace in their homeland, France. In 2007 America discovered the verrine where it took the food scene on the West Coast by storm. The LA Times wrote an article singing the praises of this new twist in the culinary world. However, in England I have never met anyone who has heard the word verrine before.

In this section of the book I will give you a taste of some of the techniques and flavour combinations you can achieve. As with the creation of terrines, once you conquer the basics, the possibilities are endless. Verrines are the ideal entertaining food as most of the components can be assembled in advance so that you only have to add the finishing touches just before serving.

In each of my recipes I have suggested the size of glass to use. To measure, fill to the brim with water and then tip into a measuring jug. Take the reading in mls.

Cooked verrines

Cooked verrines

A cooked verrine has a real surprise and delight factor. Warm up party guests by greeting them with a hot shot of something delicious in winter. Alternatively, you can cool them down with a chilled treat in summer. Quite an unexpected welcome!

When creating your own cooked verrines think about how the textures change during the cooking process. With a verrine, you can really deliver the unexpected – for example the diced pancetta, Boursin and saffron quail's egg recipe on page 110. We crack the egg at the bottom of the verrine, build the creamy cheese layer, garnish with salty pancetta, and your guest scoops out freshly cooked egg which creates a flavour and texture explosion when combined with all the other ingredients.

Once again, all of the hard work and preparation can be done ahead of time, build the verrine and just pop in the oven as guests arrive. Or, in the case of desserts, you can put them in the oven once the main course is removed, allowing ample time for cooking.

On a health conscious note, a cooked verrine needs little or no oils as steaming is the main method of cooking and as it does not need to be demoulded.

Producing a cooked verrine

Ovenproof glass
To make a cooked verrine be sure that you use ovenproof glass or pyrex dishes.

To build a verrine
Layer the different ingredients into the glass gently and smooth each layer with the back of a teaspoon. When the layering is finished tap the glass gently on a dry cloth on the table to settle the ingredients.

Bain-marie
Place a tea towel on the bottom of the roasting tin which you are using as a bain-marie. Place the heatproof verrines on the tea towel. Pour some just boiled water from the kettle up to one-third of the depth of the glasses.

Cooking
Cover the verrines in the tin with a canopy of foil to enable the them to steam gently in the oven. Do not overload the tray as the heat must circulate to make sure the verrines are evenly cooked.

Cooling
If the verrine is to be served cold, remove from the oven, then lift carefully from the bain-marie with oven gloves onto a board to cool. Allow to cool slowly. When you remove from the oven use kitchen paper to remove the steam or spills from the outside of the glass which may have occurred during the cooking.

Warning
Always make sure you are using ovenproof glass. Do not use cold water or place in the fridge to cool quickly as you may shatter the glass.

Diced pancetta with Boursin & poached quail egg

Method

1 Bring 250ml of water to the boil with the saffron strands.
2 Crack open the quail eggs and drop into a small bowl with a splash of the vinegar at the bottom.
3 When the water is boiling, take a whisk and create a whirlpool, gently tip the quail eggs and vinegar into the water and poach for 1 minute, turn off the heat and leave the eggs in the water for a further 1 minute. Remove the eggs. Skim off all of the excess egg white from the saffron water and chill. Return the eggs to the water and they will take on more of the saffron colour, leave for an hour to infuse.
4 To build, crack an egg yolk (reserving the white) into the bottom of the glass. Melt the Boursin in the microwave for 1 minute with the double cream.
5 Whisk up half of the egg white until fluffy and add to this the melted Boursin, season to taste. Add the chopped chives. Pour this mixture over the egg yolk leaving a 1cm gap to the top of the glass. Cook in a bain-marie in the middle of the oven at 180ºC, gas mark 4 for 15 minutes.
6 Dice the pancetta and fry until golden and crisp. Garnish the top of the verrine with the quail eggs, black pepper and pancetta and serve hot.

Advice

Hold the quail egg, turn it so that the fat end is pointing up. Using a serrated knife cut open the egg and tip it out. You could use turmeric instead of saffron.

Serving suggestion

Buy the long grissini, I found some wholemeal ones in my local deli.

Variation

If you can't get Boursin, you can replace this with cream cheese and add some herbs or pepper to it.

Ingredients

250ml water

1g saffron strands
(a small pinch)

18 quail eggs

2 tbsp wine vinegar

6 egg yolks

100g herby Boursin cheese

80ml double cream

sprinkle cracked black pepper

1 tsp chives, finely chopped

60g pancetta, diced

Seasoning

Preparation time
15 minutes

Cooking time
15 minutes

Serves 6 of 100ml

111

Smoked gammon with cranberries, apricots & nuts

Method

1 Dice the gammon and the apricot, mix together with the cranberry sauce and season. Spoon into the verrine and lay a bay leaf on top. Cover with a lid.
2 Cook in a bain-marie for 20 minutes at 200°C, gas mark 6.
3 Once cooked, remove the lid and discard the bay leaf. Garnish with the flaked almonds.

Advice

I have used a verrine with a lid. If you don't have a lid, tin foil will work well too.

Serving suggestion

Serve with a fine cranberry tuille (see page 194).

Variation

This is delicious for a Christmassy dinner – you could also use meats such as venison or duck.

Ingredients

280g smoked gammon ham

100g dried apricots, diced

80g cranberry sauce

4 bay leaves

15g of flaked almonds to garnish

Seasoning

Preparation time
20 minutes

Cooking time
20 minutes

Serves 4 of 100ml

Light grey mullet mousse with fresh cooked mussels

Method

1 Blitz the mullet with lemon juice, cream and seasoning.
2 Blanch the broccoli florets and then cut in half, place in the glass with the flat face to the glass. Fill inside the glass with the mullet mix. Fill the glasses to a third.
3 Cook in a bain-marie for 10 minutes at 200ºC, gas mark 6.
4 In a wok with olive oil, cook the onion with a splash of white wine, add the mussels. Slowly cook the mussels for 5–8 minutes, covered. Discard any that do not open. Remove most from the shells, reserving some for garnish.
5 To serve, top with a few long flakes of Parmesan shavings and the fresh dill leaves.

Advice

Cook the mussels while the broccoli and grey mullet are cooking, assemble and serve hot.

Serving suggestion

Delicious with simple rustic bread and Brittany salty butter.

Variation

Works very well with fresh cockles in place of mussels.

Ingredients

150g grey mullet, boned

1 tbsp fresh lemon juice

1 head broccoli

100ml double cream

Splash white wine

1 tbsp olive oil

1 tbsp white onion, diced

250g fresh, live mussels (approx 100g of cooked mussels without shell)

90g Parmesan cheese

A few dill leaves for garnish

Preparation time
15 minutes

Cooking time
10 minutes

Serves 4 of 150ml

Diver caught scallops with kipper, fennel & spinach

Method

1 Blitz the kipper with 100ml cream, egg and seasoning.

2 Place a layer of this mixture into each glass and cook in a bain-marie for 15 minutes at 200°C, gas mark 6.

3 Sweat down the spinach in a pan and add the remaining cream, season and combine. Blitz half the spinach into a sauce and leave the rest whole for added texture.

4 Remove the scallops from the shells and slice through the middle of each. Seal each side for 1 minute in a hot pan with a little olive oil. Squeeze lemon juice over them.

5 Remove the verrines from the oven, pour over the spinach sauce and build with the scallop and spinach. Serve hot.

Advice

If you prepare the ingredients (such as removing scallops from the shells) you should be able to cook the scallops and spinach while the kipper cooks. This allows the dish to come together in good time to serve hot.

Serving suggestion

Serve with a fennel wafer (see page 198).

Variation

Use queen scallops if you cannot find the diver ones, these are smaller but just as good and you can often find them frozen.

COOKED **VERRINES**

Ingredients

100g kipper fillet

140ml double cream

1 egg

Seasoning

Handful baby leaf spinach (approx 120g)

8 scallops

2-3 tbsp olive oil

1 lemon, juiced

Preparation time
15 minutes

Cooking time
15 minutes

Serves 4 of 300ml

Sweet potato & carrots with orange juice & cumin

Method
1 Peel and segment the orange.
2 Peel and dice the carrots and sweet potato, make sure they are all the same size. Layer into the verrine with the carrots at the bottom and season to taste. Arrange the segments of orange on top.
3 Sprinkle over the cumin seeds and add a chunk of butter.
4 Squeeze the remaining orange into each before closing.
5 Completely seal the verrine with a lid or tightly wrapped foil.
6 Cook for 30 minutes at 200ºC, gas mark 6.
7 For a garnish, take a fine slice of courgette, including the skin, cut to a julienne and quickly blanch.

Advice
Press the carrots and sweet potato firmly into the verrine to really fill it, as they will reduce in volume during the cooking.

Serving suggestion
Serve with a savoury shortbread (see page 195). Works as an accompaniment to meat or fish as a main course.

Variation
You could use butternut squash instead of, or as well as, the sweet potato.

Ingredients

1 orange, large

2 carrots, large

1 sweet potato

Sprinkle cumin seeds

60g salted butter

1 courgette, julienne cut

Seasoning

Preparation time
15 minutes

Cooking time
30 minutes

Serves 6 of 250ml

Cauliflower purée, creamy peas & black truffle flakes

Method

1 Chop and cook the cauliflower, the peas and the potatoes in salted water.

2 Take a wide mesh sieve and using the back of a spoon press through the peas, cauliflower and potatoes separately. Once mashed divide half of the potato between the peas and cauliflower. Mix the cream, egg and butter and add half to each of the mixes.

3 Build the layers in the verrine and tap the dish on the table to get a flat level and to remove the air bubbles.

4 Cook for 20 minutes in a bain-marie at 200°C, gas mark 6. Prior to service, crush the wasabi peas and add the sliced black truffle.

Advice

The vegetables are much easier to mash if you cook them thoroughly. You can buy wasabi peas in any good deli. I order mine online, they are sweet and not as fiery as the wasabi paste you would usually find with sushi.

Serving suggestion

Great served with a hot shot of coco blanc beans with a drizzle of truffle oil (see page 199) and a sprinkle of rock salt.

Variation

When using truffle it is preferable to use a very smooth and delicate texture like cauliflower, you could also use broccoli in place of the peas, but in a verrine always consider the colour contast.

Ingredients

150g cauliflower

150g frozen peas

80g potatoes

90ml double cream

1 egg

50g melted butter

30g dried wasabi peas

10g black truffle finely sliced

Preparation time
20 minutes

Cooking time
20 minutes

Serves 3 of 200ml

Apples in honey with fresh grapes & treacle top

Method

1 Cut the grapes in half and soak in the Cointreau.
2 Peel and cut the apples into a chunky dice. Melt the sugar in a frying pan, add the apples and toss to make sure they are covered in a light coloured caramel.
3 Add the grapes and Cointreau then arrange in the verrine.

For the topping: **1** Gently heat all of the ingredients until combined, adding the biscuit crumbs at the end. This mix goes hard once cooled so you must be are ready to add the topping before making it. Using a pallet knife press the topping onto the apple mixture.
2 Cook in the oven for 15 minutes at 180ºC, gas mark 4 in a bain-marie. Garnish with a baby apple.

Advice

Use a pallet knife to press on the treacle topping, it gives a good flat surface to garnish.

Serving suggestion

Serve with home made honeycomb (page 197). I have also garnished with tinned mini apples which are available in delis and from many online stores.

Variation

You can use other varieties of apple, whatever is in season. Or use cider or Calvados in place of Cointreau for a stronger flavour.

Ingredients

200g green grapes

3 tbsp Cointreau

250g apples, Golden Delicious

50g sugar

For the topping

75ml golden syrup

Pinch ground ginger

Splash lemon juice

50g toffee sauce

40g biscuit crumbs

Preparation time
15 minutes

Cooking time
20 minutes

Serves 5 of 110ml

Lemoncello & pistachio crème brûlée

Method

1 Bring cream to the boil.
2 Whisk the egg yolks, caster sugar, Lemoncello and salt together. Slowly add the cream.
3 Place the pistachios in the bottom of the glass and fill to the top with mixture.
4 Cook in a bain-marie at 140ºC, gas mark 3 for 40 minutes.
5 Just prior to serving, generously sprinkle over the brown sugar and use a blowtorch or the grill to burn the top.

Advice

I think brûlées are better when they are left to rest over night in the fridge but remember to leave burning the top until you are ready to serve.

Serving suggestion

Serve with fine nutty biscuits (see page 196).

Variation

Raspberries would work really well with the lemon too.

Ingredients

200ml double cream

2 egg yolks

50g caster sugar

2tbsp Lemoncello liqueur

1g salt

20g pistachio nuts

2tsp brown sugar for the topping

Preparation time
10 minutes

Cooking time
40 minutes

Chilling time
10 minutes

Serves 3 of 100ml

Set verrines

Set verrines

A set verrine is mainly achieved using aspic or gelatine but it can also use butter, fat or natural bonding ingredients found in food such as in the pig trotters (see page 135).

The main idea of a set verrine is to set ingredients into a glass using a hot or warm liquid or mix. Once set I garnish the verrine with 'loose' items to give good variation of textures.

The beauty of this technique is to achieve colourful and mouth watering flavours. A set jelly doesn't need to be clear, use the gel to hold an additional level of flavour. For example, I have used a watermelon jus to set radish in one recipe and orange juice for another.

Do be cautious about the level of gelatine you use in verrines. Remember that these will not be demoulded so they don't need to be super set. I would use just enough to fix the layers and to give a nice texture – too much will result in a chewy consistency.

Producing a set verrine

Prepare the ingredients
When blanching or cooking vegetables, remember to drain and then dry them on paper towels to remove as much excess moisture as possible. Any additional water will weaken the jelly and may prevent it from setting. You can do the setting part of the verrine in advance, to allow you to take time in layering or making the verrine. I would leave any topping or garnish until just ready to serve so that you present the freshest food to your guests.

Gelatine usage
Make sure the gelatine is fully dissolved or you may leave unpleasant, rubbery patches throughout the verrine.

Setting times
Setting time can be as little as just 30 minutes but remember you can prepare the day before to be sure.

Storage
You can keep a set verrine in the fridge for 2 days, keep it covered to be sure other contents in the fridge do not taint the flavours or dry out the top. Always garnish at the last minute.

Texture and flavour
In creating set verrines, think about how the jelly will work with the food you intend to set into it, for instance use soft, delicate fish pieces or maybe fresh crunchy veg or tender pieces of meat. Think also about how you can use the jelly as the base of flavours and how these would compliment the main ingredients used.

Poached huss with beans & slow roasted tomatoes

Method

1 Remove the fish bone from the centre of the fish and dice the flesh into cubes about 1cm square.

2 Bring the fish stock to the boil, simmer and cook the fish for 5 minutes.

3 Cut the tomatoes in half, cook them face up in a hot oven at 200°C, gas mark 6 for 5 minutes with a drizzle of olive oil and a pinch of salt. Remove from the oven and sprinkle over the black sesame seeds.

4 Use the fish stock to blanch the French beans. Remove and reduce the fish stock by half and melt in the soaked and squeezed gelatine leaves.

5 In a bowl, mix the diced fish with the tarragon and season.

6 Mix the beans with a little of this stock too.

7 Build the verrine using alternative layers of fish and beans but do allow time for the individual layers to set, this will take about 10 minutes per layer if you set in the freezer. In the centre of the verrine, spoon in a layer of the tomato purée and garnish with a tomato on top.

Advice

There is only one bone running through the centre of huss. To remove it, slice gently length ways across the back.

Serving suggestion

Serve with spinach and ricotta wafer (see page 197).

Variation

Huss is a very smooth and delicate fish, for a stronger flavour you could use tuna steaks.

Ingredients

300g huss

700ml fish stock

4 cherry tomatoes

Drizzle olive oil

Sprinkle black sesame seeds

Seasoning

150g French beans

2 gelatine leaves

1 tsp tarragon, chopped

1 tbsp tomato puree, diluted in 2 tbsp of water

Preparation time
20 minutes

Setting time
1 hour

Serves 4 of 220ml

131

Tuna & marlin set in a light jelly topped with fresh salsa

Method

For the salsa: Finely dice all of the ingredients and season to taste with olive oil at the end.

1 Dice the fish into 1cm squares and poach in the lemon juice, water and white wine for 5 minutes.
2 Remove the fish and bring the liquid to the boil.
3 Add the soaked and squeezed gelatine leaf and the chopped water cress. Return the fish to the mix and season to taste.
4 Mix all components together and arrange in glasses. Allow to set and garnish with the salsa.

Advice

Don't fill the glass too much as you will need some space for the salsa. Dress the glass with the salsa at the last minute.

Serving suggestion

Serve with a glass of chilled white Chardonnay and bread with salty butter. I love Brittany butter with the crystals of salt in.

Variation

You could use skate and capers in this recipe in place of the marlin.

Ingredients

For salsa

50g red onion

50g coriander

50g tomato

Drizzle olive oil

Seasoning

For verrine

150g tuna steak

150g marlin

1 lemon, juiced

150ml water

90ml white wine

2 gelatine leaves

4 tbsp watercress, chopped

Seasoning

Preparation time
15 minutes

Chilling time
1 hour

Serves 3 of 180ml

Pig's trotters, roasted pak choi & pickled onions

Method

1 To make the stock, cover the trotters with water and add the flavouring ingredients. Cook the trotters in the stock for 2 to 2.5 hours on a low heat.

2 While still hot, remove the bone and dice the meat. Cover with the cooking stock, add the chopped flat leaf parsley and season to taste. Set into the verrine.

3 In a pan, heat a little olive oil. Cut the pak choi in half and add it to the pan with the inside facing down. Cover with foil and cook for 5 minutes.

4 Remove from the heat and leave covered for a further 5 minutes to finish the cooking.

5 You can serve the pak choi topping hot or cold and garnish with sweet pickled onions.

Advice

Cut through the root to keep the pak choi held together for a better presentation. Serve the verrine warm, not cold as it sets too hard.

Serving suggestion

In this recipe I have used pickled onions but other pickled vegetables will work well with the gelatine in this verrine.

Variation

If you cannot find pig's trotters you could use pig's ears. Treat in the same way and then cut them into julienne as they are also naturally rich in gelatine.

Ingredients

4 pig's trotters, medium

10g rock salt

1 litre water flavoured with 8 juniper berries, handful tarragon and 8 bay leaves

2 tbsp parsley, flat leaf

3 pak choi, cut in 2

90g sweet pickled onions

Drizzle oilve oil

Seasoning

Preparation time
30 minutes

Chilling time
1 hour

Serves 6 of 225ml

135

Tagliatelle of vegetables set in an orange dressing

Method

1 Deseed all of the peppers and cut into julienne strips, blanch in salted boiling water for 10 seconds, drain immediately and dry on paper towel.

2 Use the same water for the asparagus (cut length ways into quarters and then halve the batons) and the julienne of carrot.

3 Bring the orange juice to the boil and dissolve the soaked and squeezed gelatine into it.

4 Toss all cooked vegetables with olive oil, ginger and seasoning.

5 To build, gently fill the glasses with the vegetables, don't press this down. Pour over the orange juice mix and garnish with a few sprigs of lavender.

Advice

Its good to prepare this mix ahead of the time you need it and store it in a sealed container in the fridge as it allows the flavours to blend. Fill the verrine at the last minute to delay the dressing filtering to the bottom.

Serving suggestion

Serve with croutons to give a crunch.

Variation

For an Asian twist, add some julienne of pickled ginger (the kind you would use in sushi making) and some black onion seeds to the mix of vegetables.

Ingredients

1/2 yellow pepper

1/2 red pepper

1/2 green pepper

4 asparagus spears

1 small carrot, peeled

1 pinch dried lavender for garnish

2 tbsp olive oil

1 pinch ginger powder

1 orange, juiced

1/2 gelatine leaf

Seasoning

Preparation time
25 minutes

Serves 8 of 80ml

Ratatouille set in Sauternes jelly, with tapenade

Method

1 Soak the gelatine and squeeze, whisk into 100ml of boiling water add the white wine and keep to one side.

2 To make a tomato coulis, mix the tomato purée with 40ml of water, season and reserve.

3 Roughly dice the courgette and aubergine, keeping them separate. You are aiming for about 2cm cubes. Cut the tomatoes into 8.

4 Heat the olive oil until smoking and cook first the aubergine, then the courgette, finishing with the tomato. Season to taste and then add the thyme.

5 Fill glasses to the top and slowly pour the gelatine over, make sure it filters down to the bottom by tapping on the table. Finish with a layer of tomato coulis and place in the fridge to set.

6 To make the tapenade, blitz the black olives and add a splash of olive oil and seasoning. For the garnish, dry out some fine strips of tomato peel in the oven for around 1 hour at 100ºC, gas mark 1/4.

Advice

For a perfect texture and taste the vegetables should be fully cooked through. If you don't want to darken them using the pan, transfer to a bowl and cover with cling film, the residual heat will finish the cooking by steaming.

Serving suggestion

I would add a sprinkle of rock salt just prior to serving.

Variation

You could use root vegetables and then replace the white wine with red.

Ingredients

1/2 gelatine leaf

100ml water

50ml Sauternes white wine

60g tomato purée

1/2 aubergine

1 courgette

10 cherry tomatoes

1 tsp fresh thyme, chopped

50g black olives

20ml olive oil

40ml water

Seasoning

Preparation time
25 minutes

Chilling time
30 minutes

Serves 8 of 80ml

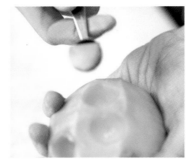

Red radish & mange-tout in watermelon jus

Method

1 Finely slice the radish and keep in cold water.
2 Peel and deseed the melons. Make fine slices with half of each melon and make melon balls with the rest. If it's a large water melon make less, as a guide about the same as the other melons.
3 Blend all of the remaining left over pieces with a hand blender and then pass through a fine sieve. Bring 450ml of the juice to a simmer with the chilli sauce and the soaked and squeezed leaves of gelatine. Whisk until dissolved. Cool down for about 10 minutes.
4 Layer in the radish and pour slowly over the liquid filling it to about a quarter of the depth of the verrine. Arrange the melon slices vertically on one side of the verrine and allow to set in the fridge. Fill with melon balls, the dried pancetta and a fine julienne of red chilli.

Advice

Make sure you use ripe melon – you should be able to smell them through the skin. This verrine is best when the melons are in season, out of season you could use citrus or soft fruits such as nectarines or peaches.

Serving suggestion

Dried Pancetta slices (see page 198).

Variation

I froze the melon balls and served them slightly defrosted which is a great cooler for a summer lunch.

Ingredients

300g radish

1 watermelon (approx 600g)

1 Charentais melon (approx 400g)

1 Galia melon (approx 400g)

1 tbsp chilli sauce

1 red chilli

3 gelatine leaves

10 fine slices of pancetta

Preparation time
30 minutes

Chilling time
30 minutes

Serves 10 of 250ml

Trio of mango, chocolate & lemon custard

Method

1 Whisk together the sugar and eggs and pour in the double cream.
2 Divide equally into three saucepans. To the first, add the lemon curd, juice and zest and heat gently, continually stirring with a spatula until it resembles scrambled eggs. With a hand blender blitz until a smooth paste and set into the verrine.
3 Repeat method 2 to make the mango purée. Make this whilst the lemon is setting and set as the middle layer.
4 Repeat method 2 using the cocoa powder blended into the cream and set on the top layer.

Advice

Don't be afraid to blitz this whilst it is still hot, the blitzing will speed up the cooling and improve the consistency too.

Serving suggestion

Serve with home made brandy snaps (see page 196).

Variation

You can make custards with other flavours, just remember to complement each of the flavours and to cook the egg mix correctly.

Ingredients

9 whole eggs

3 egg yolks

300g caster sugar

300ml double cream

For the lemon custard
1 dsp lemon curd

100ml lemon juice

10g lemon zest

For the mango
150g mango purée

For the chocolate
3 dsp cocoa
100ml double cream

Preparation time
25 minutes

Chilling time
30 minutes

Serves 6 of 200ml

143

Orange & white chocolate bavarois with florentines

Method

For the verrine: **1** Peel and cut the orange into 8 wedges. Cook and simmer for 10 minutes in 50ml of water and 30g of sugar. Allow to cool and pass through a fine sieve.

2 Gently heat the cream with the rest of the sugar. Soak and squeeze the gelatine leaves and whisk into the cream, make sure it has fully dissolved and leave to one side.

3 Melt the chocolate over a bain-marie and mix with half the double cream, mix the other half of the cream with the orange pulp.

4 Whisk the egg whites until soft peaks and divide half into each of the orange and chocolate mixture. Fold gently with a spatula to achieve a light mousse.

5 Layer the chocolate mousse into the glass, to about half way up. Lay in a few strands of prune and finish the verrine with a layer of the orange mousse. Garnish with the florentines.

For the florentines: Melt the chocolate over a bain-marie and spoon out about 1 teaspoon onto a sheet of parchment paper, creating small round disks. Whilst still hot, top with various nuts and dried fruits. Allow to cool before removing from the paper.

Advice

I would finish with the orange layer to contrast the white chocolate florentine.

Serving suggestion

Try crisp pieces of julienne of orange confit (see page 198).

Variation

Dark chocolate will also be delicious with the orange.

Ingredients

1 whole orange

70g sugar

100ml double cream

2 gelatine leaves

60g white chocolate

4 pitted prunes, fine julienne

5 egg whites

For the florentines
60g white chocolate

Few crushed nuts

Few dried apricots

Preparation time
30 minutes

Chilling time
1 hour

Serves 6 glasses of 110ml

Mousse verrines

Mousse verrines

The definition of a mousse is a chilled dessert made with cream, gelatine or eggs, a typical example would be a chocolate mousse. Although I refer to this chapter as mousse verrines, not all the recipes will be prepared with cream and eggs but we still achieve the light mousse texture.

These verrines are more suited to starters and desserts, however, you could increase the quantities to serve as a main course. As these are cold mousses, they are best enjoyed in the summer months. You could also serve something crisp like a biscuit or crunchy bread to compliment the texture.

For any verrine, but specifically a mousse verrine, it is important to keep the inside of the glass clean and to work with accuracy and precision (this comes with practice).

To produce a mousse after mastering the basics is satisfying and encourages you to create new and exciting combinations.

By using the verrine you can combine a soft, light mousse and then a layer of something crisp in texture and then top with a different mousse. The guest will fill the spoon and savour different flavour combinations on the palate.

Producing a mousse verrine

Verrine sizing

A mousse is light and full of flavour and you can really savour a small quantity. In these recipes I have not used a glass larger than 125ml, which is good portion. You could use a bigger glass for the best impact, just don't fill it.

Choosing your ingredients

When choosing your ingredients, think how you can contrast colour and texture, also use something you can blend, mix and fold into the mousse mixture – the salmon and avocado mousse on page 151 is a good example. The green and pale pink colours contrast well and I have incorporated salmon into the avocado and avocado into the salmon to add interest and texture.

Seasoning

Season and taste just before building the verrine to make sure that each layer has the correct seasoning.

Working by layers

If you intend to build your verrine in several layers, make sure you set each layer. It may take a little longer to prepare but it pays dividends in a neat end result.

Using a piping bag

I find that using a piping bag or making a cone with baking paper allows you to fill the glass neatly without smearing the sides. Pipe the contents into the glass and tap the verrine gently on the table to give it an even surface.

Storage

Chill immediately, this type of verrine will keep for 24 hours in the bottom of a cold fridge. Store covered with cling film.

Final touch

Remove the cling film and clean the outside of the glass to remove any fridge condensation. Finish with your garnish just before serving (in the case of biscuits, wafers and breads, these will go soggy if left out too long).

Smoked salmon mousse with avocado guacamole

Method

1 Reserve 40g of the smoked salmon, and blitz rest of the salmon with 1/2 of the cream cheese and 1/2 the lemon juice and zest. Season well.
2 Peel the avocado (again reserving 40g), blitz with the remaining cream cheese and lemon juice, lemon zest, Tabasco and olive oil. Season to taste.
3 Dice the reserved salmon and avocado separately, mix the salmon into the avocado mousse and the avocado dice into the salmon mousse. Keep some diced pieces to garnish.
4 Layer the various mixtures into glasses.

Advice

Use ripe avocado as they are far easier to work into a pulp and have a better flavour.

Serving suggestion

Serve with a thyme and lemon crisp (see page 196).

Variation

Other smoked fish will work well in place of the salmon, e.g. smoked trout or eel.

Ingredients

100g smoked salmon

160g cream cheese

1 lemon, juice and zest

1 avocado, medium

3 tbsp olive oil

Dash Tabasco sauce

Seasoning

Preparation time
15 minutes

Setting time
1 hour

Serves 6 of 80ml

Fresh water prawns & cucumber mousse

Method

1 Blitz together 50g of the prawns with 70g of the cream cheese, season and add a few drops of lemon juice.

2 Deseed and blitz the cucumber with the remainder of the cream cheese and season.

3 Finely dice the remaining cucumber and place in the bottom of the verrine.

4 Mix most of the whole prawns into the cucumber, sprinkle with the remaining lemon juice and fill the glass with the layers, keeping a few whole prawns for garnish.

5 Garnish with a little lumpfish roe and chopped dill just before serving.

Advice

Using a piping bag is the best way of getting the mousse into the verrines with minimum mess.

Serving suggestion

Serve with toasted granary bread.

Variation

You could use caviar if your budget is generous.

Ingredients

150g fresh water prawns, cooked

150g cream cheese

Seasoning

1 lemon, juiced

1/2 cucumber

2 tbsp black lump fish roe

1 dsp fresh dill, chopped

Preparation time
20 minutes

Serves 4 of 110ml

Smoked chicken & cream cheese with asparagus

Method

1 Finely dice the chicken and bacon.
2 Blitz the double cream and the cream cheese. Mix this with the cooked meats, add seasoning and nutmeg. Fill the glasses to a third full.
3 Blanch and cut the asparagus. Take off the tips for the top of the verrine and cut the rest of the spears into small pieces. Place on top of the cream cheese mixture.
4 Cut the tomato into quarters and deseed. Gently cut a scallop from the flesh using a round cutter to form a disk and decorate the top of the glasses.
5 Present this verrine to your guests garnished with a few leaves of thyme and a drizzle of olive oil.

Advice

When cutting the asparagus to size, measure it to the height of the verrine you are using. Be careful when adding seasoning to smoky flavours, you are aiming to enhance the flavours but beware of making the dish too salty.

Serving suggestion

Serve with a cold tomato salad dressed with olive oil, seasoning and thyme.

Variation

Smoked turkey and paprika also work well.

Ingredients

50g cooked bacon, smoked

50g smoked chicken breast

2 tbsp double cream

100g cream cheese

Good pinch nutmeg

8 asparagus spears

1 tomato

Seasoning

Thyme leaves to garnish

Drizzle olive oil

Preparation time
20 minutes

Serves 4 of 100ml

Foie gras cappuccino with quince jelly

Method

1 Put the milk into a pan with the roughly diced foie gras, add seasoning and the sugar.

2 Poach gently until the foie gras softens and begins to melt. This should take about 8 – 10 minutes.

3 Remove from the heat and pass through a sieve, discard the remaining pieces as these will be unusable.

4 Mix the cream into the foie gras milk, and transfer into a siphon whilst hot, then chill. Whilst chilling, keep shaking vigorously every 30 minutes.

5 Spray this into the verrine and garnish with the quince and a slice of black truffle. Do not spray this until just prior to service as the wonderfully delicate mousse consistency will not last too long.

Advice

You may need to order a whole lobe of foie gras from your butcher – I find it freezes really well, so cut it into portions and wrap well to keep until next time.

Serving suggestion

Serve with toasted brioche bread soldiers (see page 197).

Variation

You could use goose foie gras.

Ingredients

225ml milk

150g duck foie gras

Seasoning

Good pinch of sugar

50ml cream

6 fine slice black truffle

100g quince jelly

5g rock salt

Seasoning

Preparation time
20 minutes

Cooking time
10 minutes

Setting time
2 hours

Serves 8 of 80ml

Beetroot purée with a green bean salad

Method

1 Dice the baby leeks and green beans to the same size and cook.

2 Peel and roughly dice the beetroot and roast in a little oil for 30 minutes at 220ºC, gas mark 7. Once cooled, blitz to a purée and fold into the whipped double cream and season.

3 Take the raw shallots and cut to a julienne, deep fry in hot oil until a golden colour and drain on kitchen paper to remove excess oil.

4 Place the beetroot at the bottom of the glass, making a nest for the green beans & leeks to sit in. Garnish with the radish, fried shallots and the cress.

5 Slice a raw beetroot into wafer thin slice for crisps. Slowly dry out between 2 pieces of kitchen paper and press out the moisture. Plunge into a deep fat fryer until crisp and remove and drain on kitchen paper. Serve with the salad.

Advice

Make sure that the beetroot is well cooked so that it purées easily. To test, poke it with a knife, if still too hard, cook for a further 10 minutes but cover in foil to finish cooking by steaming.

Serving suggestion

Serve with a mango & chilli dressing (see page 192).

Variation

You could use blanched spring onions in place of the leeks.

Ingredients

180g baby leeks

180g green beans

180g raw beetroot

2tbsp olive oil

100g double cream, whipped

80g julienne of radish

50g shallots

1 punnet mustard cress

Season to taste

Preparation time
20 minutes

Cooking time
40 minutes

Serves 5 of 110ml

Sun-dried tomato, goats cheese & rocket

Method

1 Remove the skin of the goat's cheese and discard. Make a mix with the goats cheese, cream cheese and milk. To help it bind, warm gently over a bain-marie. Whisk then season to taste.

2 Split this mixture into 2 bowls, add rocket to one and half of the sun-dried tomatoes to the other.

3 Build the verrine in layers, using the sun-dried tomato pieces in between each layer.

4 Finish with roasted macadamia nuts on top, a few leaves of rocket and a fine dried slice of tomato. To make the dried tomato slices, I use a dehydrator machine. Cut the tomatoes into slices and dry in the machine for about 2 hours. Alternatively, you could use an extra bought sun-dried tomato to garnish.

Advice

Tall thin shot glasses are perfect for this recipe.

Serving suggestion

Serve with warm rosemary and tomato toasted focaccia bread.

Variation

Split the mix into 3 and add a third layer such as black olives or marinated green olives to add more texture and colour.

Ingredients

100g goat's cheese

100g cream cheese

50ml milk

Seasoning

2 tbsp chopped rocket leaves (and a few extra for garnish)

100g chopped sun-dried tomatoes

50g macadamia nuts

1 tomato, finely sliced for drying

Preparation time
20 minutes

Cooking time
10 minutes

Serves 4 of 100ml

161

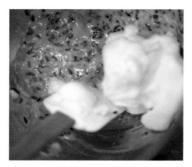

Thyme & lavender mousse with cherries

Method

1 Put 125ml of double cream and 1 tbsp of sugar separately into two saucepans. Bring to a simmer and add the lavender to one and the thyme to the other.

2 Soak and squeeze the gelatine leaf and add half to each pan, remove from the heat and transfer to 2 bowls.

3 Whisk the egg whites to soft peaks, put half into each bowl and gently mix in with a spatula or metal spoon.

4 Build the verrine using two piping bags and carefully add some cherry jam between each layer.

5 Set in the fridge for 1 hour.

Advice

Don't mix the eggs too much, a gentle folding action with a metal spoon or spatula keeps the mixture as light as possible.

Serving suggestion

Serve with parsnip ice cream (see page 199).

Variation

These flavours are both rather strong so you could substitute one of them for vanilla, it's less adventurous but also less risky if you have lots of people for dinner.

Ingredients

250ml double cream

2 tbsp sugar

1tsp dried lavender

1tsp dried thyme

1 gelatine leaf

2 egg whites

80g cherry jam

Preparation time
20 minutes

Chilling time
1 hour

Serves 8 of 100ml

Pineapple & strawberry with candied basil leaf

Method

1 Peel the pineapple and remove the stalks from the strawberries, roughly chop both into pieces.

2 Take 2 pans with 50ml water and 50g of sugar in each one, and add the pineapple to one and the strawberries to the other. Heat on the stove and boil for 5 minutes.

3 Divide the egg white into two separate bowls. Whisk the egg whites in each bowl into firm peaks.

4 Soak and squeeze the gelatine leaf and melt 1/2 into each of the hot fruit syrups.

5 Remove the fruit from the heat and transfer to a mixing bowl. Using a hand blender, you can purée to a sauce consistency, this will allow the mixture to cool.

6 Whip up the double cream until stiff.

7 Mix half the egg whites and then half the cream into each fruit.

8 Using a piping bag, gently pipe the mousses into a verrine, using basil syrup between each layer and finish with a thin layer of strawberry purée.

Advice

Use ripe fruits, they don't have to look good on the outside as you are going to blitz them. However, cut off any brown or damaged pieces.

Serving suggestion

I have separated the layers with a basil fruit syrup and crystallised a leaf of basil for the garnish.

Variation

You could use passion fruit instead of pineapple for a bitter, sharper taste.

Ingredients

125g pineapple

125g strawberries

100ml water

100g sugar

3 egg whites

1 gelatine leaf

100ml double cream

50ml basil syrup
(see page 206)

80ml strawberry purée

Preparation time
20 minutes

Cooking time
5 minutes

Chilling time
1 hour

Serves 4 of 125ml

Flowing verrines

Flowing verrines

Some may say that flowing verrines are just a salad in a glass, and I confess I am not totally in disagreement.

However, verrines bring further benefits, for instance you can prepare in advance and be ready to serve guests, you have portion control, there's no mess on the buffet or table as people dig into a large salad bowl. I think in terms of flavour, the verrine can assist in enhancing this as the dressing will act as a marinade for the salad and the flavour will be encased in the glass.

When creating flowing verrines, I think it's important to think about a mixture of textures and how these come together. Also consider how you make it a meal in a glass, so incorporate fish or meat and top with a crouton or biscuit.

Think about different ways of treating the ingredients to bring as much life and excitement into the glass, for instance chargrill some vegetables, poach some soft delicate fish or add in some crunchy crostini.

Flowing verrines work particularly well on a buffet table. Not only can you be confident you have enough to feed all your guests you don't have the worry of a sadly mauled salad bowl you took time preparing left limply on the table.

I rest easy when making a buffet knowing I have enough for everyone to eat and there's a wow factor a salad bowl can never deliver.

Producing a flowing verrine

Choosing your glass
A salad has more volume than a mousse and as we want to keep it loose and not squash or cram in the ingredients, choose a glass up to 300ml.

Ingredients
A flowing verrine will generally be eaten with a fork or a spoon (not both), so your ingredients need to be firm and bite-sized, not too large and clumsy. I would advise cutting all of your ingredients to a similar size so that they are easily speared or scooped out. If you choose to use larger pieces for one component, I would place this on top for maximum presentation effect.

Seasoning
Mix all of the ingredients in a bowl first and season before putting into the verrine – it's just not possible to distribute the seasoning well if your food is already in the glass.

Building the verrine
To keep the verrine as neat as possible fill slowly using a spoon and avoid contact with the inside of the glass or you will smear the glass with the ingredients. Allow the ingredients to arrange themselves naturally in the glass and don't try to handle them too much to create perfect layers.

Storage
Once built, I recommend storing in the fridge for a maximum of 2 hours. Much longer and the dressing will drain to the bottom and will not be as fresh and light.

Last touch
Very often fresh salads are presented with fresh aromatic herbs left whole or chopped. Keep herbs fresh by storing the stems in cold water and add them at the last minute.

Carpaccio of halibut with purple cress salad

Method

1 Cut the halibut into very thin slices and marinate in the juice of half a lemon and seasoning, leave to stand for 1 hour.
2 Peel and deseed the tomatoes and cut into a dice. Dice the green chilli and spring onion and mix them with the tomato and purple cress.
3 Toss the salad with the remainder of the lemon juice, the olive oil and the seasoning. Fill the glasses with the salad and add the halibut on top.

Advice

Buy really fresh fish for this one, keep at the bottom of the fridge and use when very cold as you will get more even slices.

Serving suggestion

Keep this verrine refrigerated, once prepared, until ready to serve. Delicious served with a glass of chilled Chardonnay.

Variation

You could use other fish like salmon or tuna. Make sure that the fish is fresh and sliced very finely to allow the lemon juice in the marinade to 'cook' it.

Ingredients

80g halibut

1 lemon

Seasoning

2 plum tomatoes, diced

1 tsp green chilli, fine diced

1 tsp chopped spring onions

3 punnets purple salad cress

10ml olive oil

Preparation time
15 minutes

Serves 3 of 300ml

Mediterranean prawn salad with sesame dressing

Method

For the verrine: **1** Peel the cooked prawns and cut all the other ingredients into chunky pieces, or wedges, approx 3cm x 3cm. Toss in olive oil, soy sauce and season with cracked black pepper and salt.

2 Sear on a very hot griddle pan to achieve the chargrill lines and transfer to a roasting tin in the oven to cook through.

3 Chill the vegetables and prawns before building the verrine

4 Layer in the vegetables placing the prawns on top and pour over the dressing.

For the dressing: Spoon the crème fraîche into a bowl and mix with all the other ingredients.

Advice

Make sure your vegetables are well cooked, you could always transfer them to an airtight container and the steam will finish the cooking.

Serving suggestion

Delicious served with freshly made blinis at a picnic on a summer day.

Variation

Use cooked mussels to mix into the vegetables and replace the dressing with a lemon and coriander dressing.

Ingredients

8 cooked large prawns

100g courgette

100g tomatoes

100g red onions

100g aubergine

100g spring onion

80ml olive oil

1 tsp soy sauce

Sprinkle cracked black pepper

Pinch of salt

For the dressing

1 tspn black sesame seeds

1 tspn honey

1 tspn crème fraîche

50ml sesame oil

40ml warm water

Preparation time
25 minutes

Serves 4 of 250ml

Bocconcini mozzarella, Parma ham & parmesan

Method

1 Cut the tomatoes in two and place on a tray lined with baking parchment with finely sliced garlic and thyme. Drizzle the olive oil over the tomatoes and season.

2 Slow cook in the oven for 2 hours at 100ºC, gas mark 1/4.

3 Cut the mozzarella and the balsamic onions in half and season.

4 To make the Parma ham crisp, lay the fine slices of ham on a lined oven tray and place a second piece of parchment on top, with a second tray on top of this, to keep it flat.

5 Dry the Parma ham in the oven for 8 to 10 minutes at 160ºC, gas mark 3.

6 To build the verrine, start with the mozzarella and onions, top with the tomatoes. Garnish with the Parma ham and the Parmesan shavings and finally drizzle with olive oil.

Advice

Season the mozzarella well as it has an excellent texture but is mild in flavour. Use a good quality extra virgin olive oil,

Serving suggestion

To make fresh garlic bread, rub garlic cloves over a baguette and toast. Alternatively, there are good frozen garlic breads available to buy.

Variation

Use feta cheese and olives in place of the mozzarella and garlic, you can also buy marinated feta cheese cubes.

Ingredients

9 cherry tomatoes

1 garlic clove

3 sprigs of fresh thyme

3 tbsp extra virgin olive oil

9 bocconcini mozzarella

9 balsamic onions

3 slices Parma ham

90g Parmesan shavings

Seasoning

Preparation time
25 minutes

Cooking time
2 hours

Serves 6 of 80ml

175

Aromatic crispy duck with a pea salad

Method

1 Trim the duck breast and remove the skin. Cut once through the duck breast length ways. Cut into thin scallops (above left) of a maximum of 5mm.
2 Quickly seal the duck in a very hot, smoking pan for about 1 minute on each side.
3 While the duck is in the pan, deglaze with a splash of soy sauce. Remove from the heat and stir in 1 tbsp of hoi sin sauce, transfer to a bowl to rest, sprinkle with seasoning.
4 Make the tahini dressing by mixing the tahini with lemon syrup, coriander and seasoning.
5 Mix the peas and the chick peas together with half of the tahini dressing.
6 Spoon this mix into your serving verrine. On top of this arrange the duck, spoon over any remaining cooking juices and a further drizzle of tahini dressing. Garnish with a hibiscus flower.

Advice

I have used the hibiscus flower to garnish this dish even though they are quite hard to find. It is well worth persevering as they come in a wonderful syrup which is great when added to Champagne. The internet is a great kitchen assistant!

Serving suggestion

Present to your guests with chopsticks for authenticity.

Variation

Finely slice scallops of pork with a sweet and sour sauce will work in place of the duck and hoi sin sauce.

Ingredients

1 duck breast (approx 300g)

1 tbsp oil

1 tbsp soy sauce

2 tbsp hoi sin sauce

Seasoning

4 tsp tahini

2 tbsp lemon syrup (see page 204)

75g chick peas

75g cooked peas

1 tsp coriander, roughly chopped

Preparation time
25 minutes

Serves 4 of 100ml

Greek salad á la verrine

Method

1 Deseed the cucumber and cut long ways into quarters, dice into cubes. Cube also the feta, tomatoes and red onions.
2 Toss the prepared vegetables with the olive oil, fresh thyme and seasoning.
3 Present in the verrine as loose as possible, don't push down into the glass, let the vegetables drop in, keep it simple and serve straight away.

Advice

This is a very basic recipe, and here I am trying to show how you can be creative using different combinations of salad. Just make sure you don't crush or bruise the ingredients you use.

Serving suggestion

This verrine would work well as a side salad accompaniment with grilled meats, fish or even for a barbeque.

Variation

I have balled my vegetables with a melon scoop but this dish works equally well when the ingredients are diced neatly and evenly.

Ingredients

1 cucumber, medium

100g feta cheese

25g pitted black olives

10 cherry tomatoes, ripe

1 red onion, medium

2 tbsp olive extra virgin oil

1 tsp fresh thyme

Seasoning

Preparation time
15 minutes

Serves 5 of 100ml

Duck confit with marinated figs & fresh coriander

Method

1 Cook the duck slowly in the fat for 2 hours on a low heat. Allow to cool and shred.

2 Cut the figs in half, julienne the spring onion and grate the carrots. Dress each of these individually with olive oil and seasoning.

3 Put half of the shredded duck at the bottom of the glasses and add the fig quarters.

4 Arrange the remaining vegetables and then top with the other half of the duck and figs on the top.

5 Tightly wrap a plate with cling film and brush over a layer of olive oil. Take each individual coriander leaf and 'stick' it to the cling film. Microwave on full power for 90 seconds, the result is a flat, fried leaf to use as a garnish.

Advice

Don't be put off by the amount of fat used in cooking the duck, you can reserve and reuse for instance in roasting potatoes. Allow the duck to cool in the fat, this keeps the meat moist, tender and full of flavour.

Serving suggestion

Serve with filo forks (see page 198).

Variation

You could use chicken livers cut into fine scallops and cooked in goose fat.

Ingredients

2 duck legs, raw

250g duck fat

10 baby marinated figs

1 tbsp chopped spring onion

1 medium carrot

10ml olive oil

Seasoning

Preparation time
15 minutes

Cooking time
2 hours

Serves 4 of 300ml

Cherry, figs & raspberries in port & orange vinegar

Method
1 Pour the port, juice of 1 orange and 2dsp of sugar into a saucepan. Heat and reduce by half on a medium heat.
2 Cut the figs into quarters.
3 Put the raspberries into melted butter and roll them around to get a good coverage. Coat half with biscuit crumb and the other half in crushed pistachio nuts.
4 Add the figs and the cherries to the warm reduced syrup and toss to cover. Gently soften the fruit without cooking.
Build the verrine and pour over any remaining cooking port juice.

Advice
Don't overcook the fruit, just allow to be slightly soft.

Serving suggestion
I have used a chemistry pipette for serving the sauce – it's this kind of thing that will really surprise your guests and get the conversation flowing!

Variation
You could use strawberries, rhubarb or blackcurrants.

Ingredients

8 dsp port

1 orange

2 dsp sugar

4 fresh figs

125g raspberries

250g fresh cherries

50g butter

3 dsp biscuit crumbs

3dsp crushed pistachio nuts

Preparation time
15 minutes

Serves 8 of 110ml

Pear poached in beetroot jus & roasted plums

Method

1 Peel and dice the beetroot and just cover with water – simmer for 15 minutes, covered. Remove and discard the beetroot, but keep the cooking liquid.

2 To the cooking liquid add sugar and cinnamon and bring back to the boil for 2 minutes.

3 Peel and core the pears and cut each into 8 wedges, poach in the beetroot jus for 5 minutes and leave to cool in the pan.

4 Cut the plums in half and remove the stones. Cut into 8 wedges and place in a bowl. Sprinkle with icing sugar and ground almonds, mix well to ensure the plums are well coated. Lay on a lined baking tray and cook at 250ºC, gas mark 8 for 8 – 10 minutes, remove and allow to cool.

5 Build the verrine using the cinnamon stick as a garnish.

Advice

Don't worry if the plums get a little mushy, you can place them at the bottom of the glass, the flavour will still be good and give a different texture.

Serving suggestion

I have served this verrine with some pistachio macaroons but this is a complex recipe to perfect and I would recommend that you purchase these. If you are unable to find macaroons a shortbread biscuit would work just as well.

Variation

Use this process with diced pears and place into a glass, cover with hot mulled wine and serve to your guests on a cold winter evening.

Ingredients

2 raw beetroot, approx 300g

150g sugar

1 stick cinnamon

2 fresh William pears

250g plum, approx 4 or 5

50g icing sugar

25g ground almonds

Preparation time
20 minutes

Cooking time
15 minutes

Serves 6 of 300ml

185

Making the most of verrines

Verrines are perfect for entertaining. Not only are they beautiful to behold, but you can do all the preparation in advance and simply 'build' the verrine prior to serving so that guests enjoy the fresh tastes.

As an aperitif or canapé

Serve with drinks when guests first arrive. Verrines in a shot glass with a teaspoon to scoop up those flavours, look stunning sitting on a tray and are certainly a conversation starter. Or you could serve as a 'mis en bouche' (to get the juices going before a starter) they look great sitting on the table as guests sit down. A verrine works well at a cocktail canapé reception, Try something very light and fresh on a hot summer day or something warming on a cold day.

Dinner party

A verrine is the perfect start or finish to a dinner party, I find guests can't fail to be impressed with both the lovely presentation and the discovery of flavours. You could serve these individually to your guests with bread or a biscuit on each side plate, or present on a large tray and place in the centre of the table (like a tray of cocktails) and guests can help themselves. Do take care if you are serving a cooked verrine and the glasses are hot!

Making the most of verrines

Buffet

Portion control on a buffet and ease of service are two key considerations for me when creating a menu. My biggest fear is running out, I also hate having too much and being wasteful. A verrine is a great solution as it enables guests to 'grab' a portion and it also allows for choice if you serve meat, fish and vegetarian varieties. Make sure your guests know what you have made the verrine with, if you are not around to tell them they may miss out if they are unsure if there's something in there that they can't eat. For outdoor parties it is worth considering plastic glasses to avoid breakages.

A trio to please everyone

It is essential to offer choice when cooking for a large number of guests. Often this can mean playing it safe to keep everyone happy. My solution is to offer a trio plate as a starter or desert. This means offering three small portions of different varieties. I find guests enjoy a little sample of different flavours or, if there is something they don't like, it's easy to swap with friends.

On a buffet... my biggest fear is running out, I also hate having too much and being wasteful.

Serving suggestions

These are the recipes that accompany the terrines
or verrines. Don't just stick to my combinations mix
and match and experiment with flavours!

DRESSINGS

Pink peppercorn & lemon

50ml olive oil
50ml lemon juice
1 tsp cider vinegar
5g ground pink peppercorns
Seasoning to taste

1.Whisk together olive oil and lemon juice until it forms an emulsion (this means blended together to a creamy consistency).
2. Add cider vinegar with ground peppercorns and season to taste.
3. To make this into an ice cube, simply pour into a mould and freeze over night.

Mint and passion fruit

2 whole passion fruit
1 lemon, juiced
1 pinch ginger powder
1 pinch black onion seeds
50g sesame oil
6 leaves fresh mint
Season to taste

1. Cut the passion fruit in half and scoop the flesh out.
2. Whisk with lemon juice, sesame oil, ginger powder

and onion seeds.
3. Finely chop mint and add just prior to serving (it goes dark if added too soon).

Balsamic and cherry griottine jus

100ml balsamic vinegar
100ml cherry griotine jus
(this is the liquid from the cherry jar).

1. In a pan, bring the vinegar and cherry juice to a simmer, reduce this down to a third of the original volume and you will have a syrup.
2. Store this in a plastic bottle as it makes serving easier.

Tahini

1 tsp tahini paste
1 pinch ground ginger
1 tsp hot water
1 tsp lime juice
1 tsp olive oil
Season to taste

1. Spoon the tahini into a bowl and then, in the following order, whisk in the ginger, hot water, lemon juice, olive oil, seasoning. Whisk well and serve.

Mango & chilli

1 ripe mango
100ml sesame oil
1 tsp cider vinegar
Pinch of salt
1 tbsp chilli oil

1. Peel and dice the mango and blend to a fine puree.
2. Add the sesame oil, vinegar and salt.
3. Pass through a muslin cloth into a dish.
4. Add the chilli to taste.

SAUCES

Vanilla Sauce

1 vanilla pod
1/2 litre semi skimmed milk
30g butter
35g flour
30g sugar
Pinch of salt

1. Split open the vanilla pod, add the seeds and the pod to the milk in a pan. Place over a low heat and bring to a gentle simmer. Turn off the heat and infuse the milk for a further 5 minutes.
2. Make a roux with the butter and flour in a thick saucepan.
3. Add the milk slowly to the

roux and keep whisking, bring to the boil and then add the sugar and salt.
4. Remove the whole vanilla pod. Chill and serve.

Spicy mango syrup
25g glucose
50g water
6 drops Tabasco sauce
50g sugar
50g mango purée

1. Mix all ingredients together in a small saucepan.
2. Bring to the boil for few minutes.
3. Leave to cool and serve or store as required.

Mustard hollandaise
2 egg yolks
1 tbsp white wine
1 tsp chopped tarragon
125ml melted butter
1 tsp English mustard
Season with white pepper and table salt

1. Pour the eggs yolk, white wine, tarragon and mustard into a stainless steel bowl and heat over a simmering pan of water (there should be no direct contact with the heat).

2. Whisk briskly until foamy and remove from the heat. Slowly add the butter and keep whisking until smooth and creamy, this will take 3 to 5 minutes. Serve immediately.

Aioli emulsion
1 egg yolk
100ml olive oil
Bunch chives, chopped
1 garlic cloves finely chopped
Seasoning to taste

1. Mix egg yolk with garlic, seasoning and chives in a stainless steel bowl and heat over a simmering pan of water (there should be no direct contact with the heat).
2. Whisk briskly until foamy and remove from the heat. Slowly add the olive oil and keep whisking until cool.

Hot chocolate sauce
100g dark chocolate
150ml double cream
1 tbsp Cointreau

1. Heat the chocolate over a bain-marie.
2. Warm the cream and when the chocolate is completely melted add the cream, whisk

slowly to form a smooth consistency.
3. Add the Cointreau at the end. Transfer to a storage container, heat for 45 seconds in the microwave before serving.

Hot, dark rum sauce
60g caster sugar
40g glucose
100g water
5 tbsp rum

1. Bring the sugar, glucose and water to the boil.
2. Boil briskly for 3 minutes, add the rum.
3. Take off the heat and allow to cool.

Tip: Dip your finger in cold water before trying to remove the glucose from the tub.

Crème Anglaise
4 egg yolks
70g caster sugar
250ml semi-skimmed milk

1. Whisk the egg yolk and sugar together until foamy.
2. Bring the milk to a boil and then remove from the heat.
3. Whisk the eggs into the milk >

Serving suggestions

and bring back to a simmer again.
4. Remove from the heat. Sieve and cool down.

CHUTNEY, JAM & JELLY

Plum chutney
50g sultanas
80ml water
50g banana shallots
40g butter
4 plums, destoned
1 tsp white wine vinegar
40g dark brown sugar
1/4 tsp ground cinnamon
Seasoning to taste

1. Soak the sultanas in the water.
2. Dice the shallots and cook slowly with the butter until soft.
3. Dice the plums and add to the shallots and allow to cook for a few minutes.
4. Add the water and the sultanas, cover and simmer for a further 15 minutes.
5. Stir in the vinegar and dark brown sugar until the sugar has dissolved.
6. Stir in the cinnamon and seasoning, allow to cool and cover.

Tomato jam
3 tomatoes, diced – skin on
30g tomato puree
50g sugar
10g pectin

1. Place all ingredients into a saucepan and simmer gently for about 5 minutes. Allow to cool and chill.

Granny Smith jelly
2 Granny Smith apples
250ml water
50g caster sugar
2 gelatine leaves

1. Peel and dice the apples
2. Place in a pan with the water and sugar, cook slowly, covered for 10 minutes.
3. Blend to a paste and pass through a sieve.
4. Soak the gelatine and squeeze out the excess water.
5. Reheat the apple mixture and add the gelatine, dissolve with a whisk, leave to cool and serve.

DIPS & MAYONNAISE

Moutabal
1 aubergine
50g olive oil
1 clove garlic
1 lemon, juiced
Seasoning to taste

1. Cut the aubergine length ways in half and score the flesh.
2. Place face down in the olive oil and allow to soak for 30 minutes.

3. Using a hot griddle, cook the aubergine flesh side down for 3 minutes.
4. Chop the garlic and sprinkle over the flesh of the aubergine and place in oven to finish cooking for 15 mins at 220 C, gas mark 7.
5. Remove from the oven, cover with cling film and leave to steam for a further 15 minutes.
6. Remove the flesh and blend with the lemon juice and seasoning.

Horseradish mayo
25g fresh horseradish root
100ml white wine
150g good quality Mayonnaise
Seasoning

1. Grate the horseradish into the white wine in a saucepan, bring to the boil and reduce by one third.
2. Allow to cool and pass through a sieve.
3. Mix the remain liquid with the mayonnaise and season to taste.

Loose hummus
100g chick peas
10g garlic
40g tahini paste
150ml olive oil
3 tbsp lemon juice
50g water
Season to taste

1. Blend the ingredients together to aim for a fine paste. First blend the chick peas and garlic and then slowly add tahini paste and olive oil.
2. Season to taste with the lemon juice and water.
3. Allow to rest for 1 hour in a cool place before serving.

Pink mustard mayonnaise
2 egg yolks
15g Moutarde de Beaume
150g vegetable oil
1-2 tsp cider vinegar
Season to taste

1. Whisk egg yolk and mustard together.
2. Continue whisking, add oil slowly.
3. Keep whisking until firm. Add vinegar and season to taste.
Tip: Works with French or English mustard too.

BISCUIT, TUILLE & BREAD

Panatonne Melba toast
1. Sliced panatonne 5mm thick.
2. Roll the slice with a rolling pin and slice into the shape you like.
3. Toast in a hot oven at 220ºC, gas mark 7 until golden brown and leave to cool draped over the rolling

pin to form the shape – the sugar content will hold the shape. These do not store very easily, serve soon after making.

Biscotte
Take slices of white bread, cut off the crust. Fry until golden brown and dry at 100ºC, gas mark 1/4 in the oven for 30 minutes.

Cherry biscotti
70g glace cherries
120g blanched almonds
300g flour
200g caster sugar
5g table salt
5g baking powder
8g bicarbonate of soda
3 whole eggs

1. Preheat the oven at 220ºC, gas mark 7.
2. Sieve together the flour, sugar, salt, baking powder and bicarbonate of soda in a bowl.
3. Beat the eggs and pour onto the mix with chopped cherry and blanch almond to create a dough.
4. Line a tray with baking parchment.
5. Form into long strips 2 - 4cm thick. Lay on the parchment.
6. Cook for 15 minutes, cut into biscuits of 5mm thick and place back in the oven

for a further 5 minutes.

Cranberry tuille
2 egg whites
75g icing sugar
50g flour, sieved
50g butter
1 tsp cranberry sauce

1. Mix the egg white and icing sugar together until foamy.
2. Add the flour slowly and then add the melted butter, and the cranberry sauce at the end.
3. Put the mix in an airtight container for a minimum of 1 hour in the fridge.
4. Using a palette knife, stencil a fine layer onto a silicon mat or greased and floured baking tray.
5. Bake at 220ºC, gas mark 7 until just golden brown.
6. Remove to a wire tray to cool and then serve.

Savoury shortbread
75g butter
125g flour
Pinch of paprika
Pinch of salt
125g grated cheddar
50g grated parmesan

Make this recipe using a mixing machine or by hand.
1. Cut the butter into small pieces and mix with the flour, paprika and salt. >

195

Serving suggestions

Add the cheese at the end and form a dough.
3. Leave to rest in the fridge for 1 hour, roll to 5mm thick and cut into portions, bake at 200°C, gas mark 6, for 9-12 minutes until golden in colour.

Nutty biscuits
130g butter
300g brown sugar
90g water
180g crushed hazelnuts
60g pistachio nuts
500g flour
5g bicarbonate of soda

1. Gently melt the butter, brown sugar and water in a large saucepan.
2. Remove from the heat and mix well with the remaining ingredients.
3. Pack into a terrine mould and put in the fridge over night.
4. Demould and cut into thin slices, lay onto a non-stick tray and cook at 180°C, gas mark 4 until golden brown.

Brandy snap
60g sugar
60g golden syrup
70g butter
110g plain flour

1. Place sugar, syrup and butter in a saucepan and bring to the boil.

2. Slowly add and mix in the flour.
3. Remove from the heat, transfer to an airtight container and chill for a minimum of 2 hours.
4. Preheat the oven to 190°C, gas mark 5. Use the chilled mixture to make some balls of about 25g each.
5. Place on a greased baking tray and cook in the oven for approx 5 minutes.
6. Remove and cool draped over a rolling pin or bottle to give a good shape.

Blinis
15g fresh yeast
300ml warm milk
250g flour
60g egg yolk
15g vegetable oil
5g salt
60g melted butter
90g egg white
15g caster sugar

1. Dilute the yeast with a little of the warmed milk and add 100g of flour.
2. In another bowl mix the rest of the flour with egg yolks, milk, oil and melted butter. Mix the ingredients in both bowls.
3. Whip the egg whites until they form a soft peak and add the sugar at the end. Fold gently into the mix.
4. Leave to rest for 30

minutes to 1 hour.
5. Cook in a hot, greased pan as you would cook a small pancake.

Transparent thyme rice paper crisp
2 sheets of rice paper
1 lemon, zested
2 sprigs of thyme
1 tbsp olive oil

1. To make the crisp, soak the rice paper in cold water, remove and dry well on tissue paper.
2. Sprinkle with lemon zest and sprigs of thyme.
3. Fold in half to create a semi circle. Line a baking tin with parchment and brush with a little oil.
4. Cut the rice paper into wedges and place onto the oiled tray. Paint a second piece of paper and lay on top of the crisp with a further baking tray to flatten them as they cook.
5. Cook at 200°C, gas mark 6 for approx 5-8 minutes. Take care as they burn very easily!

Brioche bread soldiers
10g fresh yeast
1-2 tbsp water
210g flour
20g sugar
Pinch of salt
2 whole eggs

110g unsalted butter
(at room temperature)

1. Dilute the fresh yeast with a small amount of water to make a runny paste.
2. In a bowl mix together flour, sugar, salt, eggs and yeast. Add the diced butter at the end and mix the dough until the butter is fully integrated.
3. Cover the dough with cling film and leave it to prove for 1 hour at room temperature.
4. Preheat the oven to 180ºC, gas mark 4.
5. Knock back the dough and pour into a loaf tin, bake in the oven for 20-25 minutes. Leave to cool over night and cut into soldiers.

GARNISH

Frozen basil paste
8 leaf fresh basil
50ml double cream
Seasoning

1. Blanch the basil leaves for 15 seconds and cool quickly in iced water.
2. Pour the cream into a bowl, add seasoning, blend the basil with a hand blender into the cream.
3. Pass through a muslin cloth and freeze in a container. Spoon out when frozen and serve.

Crystallised sticks of rhubarb
1 stick of rhubarb
Sprinkling of icing sugar

1. With a sharp vegetable peeler take long strips from the rhubarb stick.
2. Lay the strips on a lined baking tray. With a fine sieve, sprinkle generous amounts of icing sugar over the rhubarb.
3. Place in the oven at 100ºC gas mark 1 for 30 minutes. Slowly peel the strips from the tray and turn over. Let dry for a further 15 minutes.

Honeycomb
150g water
140g caster sugar
50g honey
10g bicarbonate of soda

1. Put the water, caster sugar and honey in a pan and heat until it becomes a caramel. Remove from the heat.
2. On a heat resistant surface lay out a sheet of baking parchment.
3. Add the bicarbonate to the caramel and quickly whisk, this is very hot and will triple on volume so be very careful! Tip out onto the paper to cool. You must work quickly once the bicarbonate is added!
4. Once cold, break into pieces and serve.

Spinach & ricotta wafer
180g flour
Pinch of salt
1 tsp baking powder
2 eggs
10ml olive oil
10ml milk
200g feta cheese
100g grated gruyere cheese
3 tbsp chopped cooked spinach

1. Take 2 bowls. In the first mix together the flour, salt and baking powder.
2. In the second, whisk the eggs, olive oil and milk.
3. Pour the eggs mix into the flour and mix gently.
4. Cut the feta cheese into into 5mm squares. Add to the mix with the gruyere cheese and spinach. Pour into a lined cake tin and cook it in the oven at 180ºC, gas mark 4 for 50 minutes.
5. Cool down, turn out and freeze. While frozen cut into thin slices and lay on a sheet of baking parchment and cook for 2-3 minutes at 200ºC, gas mark 6.
6. Allow to cool down and serve, store the remainder in an airtight container. >

Serving suggestions

Fennel wafer
Finely sliced raw fennel
Olive oil

1. Lay onto a baking tray lined with parchment brush with olive oil, add another layer of paper on top and press down using a second baking tray.
2. Cook at 160°C, gas mark 3 for 20 minutes. Keep checking it as it is done when golden and dry.

Julienne of orange confit
1 orange
150g sugar
150ml water

1. Peel the orange and cut the skin into long strips. Blanch (boil water, add the orange strip and return to the boil) for one minute, discard this water and repeat twice.
2. Make a syrup using the sugar and water (boil the water and sugar for 5 minutes) add the orange and bring back to the boil.
3. Remove from the heat and allow to cool, remove the orange strips when completely cool and dry off on a piece of paper.
4. Sprinkle some sugar on a tray and toss the orange pieces until covered. Lay out on a baking tray and let them dry in the oven for 1 hour at 100°C, gas mark 1/4.

Dried pancetta or Parma ham slices
Finely sliced meats, to your requirements

1. Ask your deli to slice into thin strips.
2. Lay onto a baking tray lined with parchment, add another layer of paper on top and press down using a second baking tray.
3. Cook at 160°C, gas mark 3 for 20 minutes. Keep checking – it is done when golden and dry.

Filo forks
50g filo pastry
1 egg wash
(made with 1 egg)

1. To make a filo fork, brush a square of filo pastry with egg wash. Roll it tightly, make bristles out of one end by making small cuts.
2. Using a deep fat fryer, very carefully fry the 'handle', use tongs to keep your hands clear of the oil. Turn around and now fry the bristles, it won't take long to achieve a golden brown colour.

Fried basil leaves
1. Heat oil in a deep fat fryer to 180°C.
2. Pick single leaves of basil.
3. Plunge into the hot oil and immediately replace the lid as the water content in the leaf causes the oil to spatter.
4. When they float to the top of the oil they are ready, remove and drain on kitchen towel.

ACCOMPANIMENTS

Pickled vegetables
150g carrots
150g silver skin onions
150g cauliflower florettes
250ml cider vinegar
60g caster sugar
250ml water
10g salt
5g cracked black pepper
3 bay leaves

1. Cut all of the vegetables into bite sized chunks, but keep the onions whole.
2. Bring the cider, sugar, water, seasoning to a simmer.
3. Plunge the vegetables in and cook covered for 8 minutes.
4. Remove from the heat and allow to cool down completely before transferring into jars for storage. When cool, cover and keep in the fridge.

Fried capers, tomato and lemon concasse

1 tsp fried capers
100g chopped and deseeded tomatoes
1 lemon, zested
1 tsp olive oil
Seasoning to taste

Fry the capers and add to the chopped tomatoes and the lemon zest, stir gently in the olive oil and season to taste.

Braised salsifie

2 roots of salsifie
10g butter
2 tbsp olive oil

1. Peel the salsify and cut on the angle wedges 1 cm thick, fry in a little butter and oil until golden brown and soft.
2. Transfer to a bowl and cover with cling film to finish cooking by steaming.
3. Serve cold.

Sweet caramelised peaches

2 white peaches
50g honey
50ml balsamic vinegar

1. Remove the stone and cut each peach into 8 sections.
2. Pour the honey into a hot frying pan and heat for a few minutes until it begins to caramelise.

3. Add the peaches and toss for 20 seconds to ensure they are well coated.
4. Deglaze with the balsamic vinegar and leave to cool in the pan before serving.

Fennel & cumin confit

70g unsalted butter
20g olive oil
1 bulb fennel, diced
1 tsp cumin seeds
1 lemon, zested
Seasoning to taste

1. Heat the butter and olive oil in a saucepan over a low heat.
2. Add the diced fennel and cook slowly for 10-12 minutes.
3. Sprinkle on the lemon zest and cumin seeds. Season to taste.

Hot shot of coco blanc

100g coco blanc beans
400ml chicken stock
50ml white wine
1 small white onion, diced
Seasoning to taste
drizzle olive oil

1. Soak the beans overnight in just enough chicken stock to cover them.
2. Cook the beans in the chicken stock with white wine and onion.
3. When cooked, blitz with hand blender until very

smooth, season to taste and serve hot in a glass with a drizzle of olive oil.

Parsnip ice cream

200g parsnips, peeled
300ml milk
3 egg yolks
70g sugar
200ml double cream

1. Peel and dice the parsnip and poach in the milk to infuse.
2. Use a hand blender to blitz and pass the milk through a fine sieve.
3. Beat the eggs with the sugar and then add the infused milk slowly.
4. Cook slowly until it forms a custard consistency (test with a thermometer - at 80ºC it's done, at 81ºC it's ruined).
5. Remove from the heat and add the cold double cream. Allow this to cool completely and churn in an ice cream machine.

Technique

Here are some further explanations of the
techniques i've used throughout this book

Working with gelatine

Gelatine leaves are dehydrated and
therefore very hard. You will need to soak
them in cold water for at least 10 minutes
and squeeze out excess water. Then
dissolve them into a hot liquid, keep
whisking all of the time. Alternatively you
can buy powdered gelatine by Super Cook
(www.supercook.co.uk). One sachet is
approximately equal to 4 leaves of
gelatine (4 leaves sets 500ml, 1 sachet
sets 450ml).

Deglazing

This is the action of removing the flavours
from a hot pan or roasting tray left by a
piece of meat for instance. Add a
generous splash of wine or water to the
pan, this will loosen what's at the bottom
and make the good start to a sauce or jus.

Reducing by half

This is the action of leaving a pan on the
stove containing a liquid such as balsamic
vinegar and simmering until the liquid
evaporates and half of the starting liquid
remains. This technique is used to
produce a thicker liquid and a more
concentrated flavour.

Infusing

You can infuse flavours into any cooking
liquid. Bring water to a simmer and add
fresh mint leaves, for example, turn off the
heat and leave aside, covered to cool.

Pass through a fine sieve or muslin. The
technique of infusing is to bring colour
or flavour (or both) to a liquid.

Steaming

I often cover food with cling film or tin foil
to finish the cooking.

Muslin

Muslin is a fine cotton sheet with many
uses such as cheese making. It allows
excess liquid to slowly drain from
ingredients. This is a slow process and
best done hanging over a bowl in the
fridge over night, this ensures no solids
pass through.

Passing

Pass any stock or cooking liquid through a
chinoise or fine sieve. Just press gently
with the back of a ladle or shake the sieve
to release as much liquid as possible.

Soft peaks

Soft peaks are the result of whisking an
egg white. It is ready when the whisk
creates a soft gentle peak when removed
from the mix.

Folding

Folding is the action to slowly incorporate
two fragile ingredients – egg whites and
chocolate sauce to make a mousse for
example. With a spatula, bring in from the
side of the bowl and into the middle. >

Dice Concasse

Julienne Mirepoix

Brunoise

Technique

Defrosting

Defrosting should always take place in the fridge at a temperature between 4 to 5°C. Never in a bowl of hot water or out of the fridge.

Prepping fish

Keep a board that you will only use for fish. Work with fish quickly and efficiently to keep it cold for as long as possible.

Sweating

Cooking slowly in a saucepan with a thick bottom in a little butter and a splash of oil to prevent it from buring. Stir from time to time and remove when the vegetables have just softened or are translucent.

Bain-marie

Some terrines and verrines require steam in the oven to keep moist. Place the terrine or verrine onto the baking tray and fill to about one third. Always start this process with hot water or it slows down cooking. A bain-marie is useful for melting chocolate or for gently heating a sauce. Simmer a pan of water and use a bowl to sit it on top of the saucepan, do not allow the water to touch the bottom of the bowl.

Blanching & refreshing

Cooking quickly in salted boiling water, drain and serve if required hot. If required cold refresh in a bowl of iced water by draining the vegetables and quickly transferring them to the iced water. This action fixes the vegetable's colour and prevents residual heat from continuing to cook it.

Sauté

This is the method of cooking using hot oil and a knob of butter in a pan. Sauté potatoes are a good example of this method, add sliced potatoes to the oil and butter and cook until crisp and golden on the outside and soft and fluffy on the inside.

Poaching

Cooking in a liquid starting off cold and bringing to a simmer, often leaving the product in the liquid to cook down (but not exclusively). You get a good transmitting of flavours and colours, see the example of poached pears in beetroot (see page 185).

Searing

To scorch something with an intense heat. Useful when using a char grill to mark meat or vegetables, or when sealing a piece of meat before roasting in the oven.

Storage

It seems obvious, but always store the prepared terrines and verrines in the fridge, wrapped in cling film or in an airtight container. All dry products should be kept in a dry and well ventilated area to prevent spoiling.

Gelatine

Refreshing

Searing

Poaching

Basic recipes

Here are some core recipes you may need when making your terrines and verrines

White chicken stock
5 bay leaves
2 chicken carcasses
1 garlic clove
3 stalks of celery
2 carrots
1 medium white onion
A few sprigs of fresh thyme
Water

Method
Place all ingredients into a large pan and just cover with cold water. Bring to the boil and then leave to simmer for 1 hour. Skim the top off the liquid often. Allow to cool down and then put in the fridge. The following day remove the bones and other ingredients and pass through a fine sieve. Store in an air tight container or freeze in smaller portions to use as required.

Dark stock
Exactly the same as above, except roast the bones in a little vegetable oil first.

Making stock
If you make a large batch of stock and freeze it in small plastic containers, once frozen, you can pop it out of the container and store frozen in a bag. This way you always have stock ready when you need it and you don't have the bother of making small quantities frequently.

Lemon syrup
100g sugar
1 large lemon
Water

Method
Cut the lemon into wedges, about 10. Lay on the bottom of a saucepan. Sprinkle over the caster sugar and add water until just covering the lemons. Bring to the boil, and simmer for 5 minutes, allow to cool. Blitz with a hand blender and pass through a muslin cloth or a very fine sieve.

Alternatively you could just boil the sugar and the juice of the lemon together in a pan and pass through sieve, as a quicker marinade.

Bread crumbs
Slices of white bread

Method
Lay the slices on a rack in the oven and slowly dry out at 130°C, gas mark 1/2 for 20 minutes. Turn the oven off and leave the bread inside to cool down and >

Basic recipes

finish drying. Once dry, using a food processor blitz in to crumbs. If you need fine breadcrumbs pass through a sieve.

Caramel
30g sugar
25ml water

Method
Heat together on the stove until it melts into a dark, syrupy consistency.

Egg wash
This is an egg mixture which is brushed over pastry to give an even golden colour and finish. Whisk one egg with a splash of water and add a pinch of both sugar and salt. The salt gives the wash a richer colour.

Making a roux
A white or brown roux is made in the same way, simply cook the butter and flour until dark for brown or golden for a white base.
100g butter
125g flour
1 litre hot milk
Pinch of nutmeg
Seasoning

Method
Melt the butter and add the flour all at once. Stir and cook for a few minutes, you will know it's done when the mixture bubbles at the edge. Pour the hot milk in slowly and keep whisking all the time. Season at the end with salt, white pepper and nutmeg.

Granny Smith jelly
2 Granny Smith apples
250ml water
50g caster sugar
2 gelatine leaves

Peel and dice the apples. Place in a pan with the water and sugar, cook slowly, covered for 10 minutes. Blend to a paste and pass through a sieve. Soak the gelatine and squeeze out the excess water. Reheat the apple mixture and add the gelatine, dissolve with a whisk, leave to cool and serve.

Basil syrup
2 tsp fresh basil
(about 8 leaves)
75ml water
75g sugar

Blanch the basil leaves for 10 seconds and chop finely. Make a syrup using the water and sugar by bringing to the boil and boil for a further 5 minutes. Allow this to cool and stir in the chopped basil. Leave to infuse over night before serving.

Basic equipment

Here are some of the basic tools I use
to produce my terrines and verrines

Copper pans
Distribute the heat evenly and do
not stick. I find them particularly
useful for sugar work. They are
a bit more expensive but a
medium-sized one is a very
good investment.

Serrated knife
Very useful when cutting terrines
as it allows sawing across the
block to give a neat slice, without
squashing the terrine.

Round spatula
Use a spatula to remove mixture
from bowls and pans and save any
mixture wastage.

Temperature probe
Something I use every day in food
preparation and it's an inexpensive
investment. Always use it to test
the centre of the product. It allows
me to make sure my products are
properly and safely cooked.

Mini mixer
Ideal for chopping herbs or
chopping small quantities. Also

excellent for making small
quantities of paste, for example:
pesto or fish mousse.

Steel
A utensil for sharpening knives to
allow precision in preparation and
cutting.

Hand blender
Or a stick blender. For making
soups, sauces and emulsions.

Dehydrator
Not strictly a basic tool but great
if you have one. This is one of the
first things I purchased when
setting up my kitchen – it took a
little research on the internet to
find. I find myself using it a lot to
dry fine slices of veg, herbs and
fruits. Alternatively you can use
the oven, although it takes much
longer.

Meat slicer
Allows you to cut a very thin slice
when oven drying meat or
vegetables. This is not something
you would expect every domestic >

Basic equipment

kitchen to have but I have seen small ones on the market. If you don't have one, explain to your friendly deli or butcher what you are trying to achieve – they will help in slicing meats you are buying from them.

Sugar thermometer
Useful when making caramel, desserts and other sugar work. It will tell you exactly the different stages in the cooking of sugar and an accurate temperature.

Polystyrene
You can use polystyrene to block out a portion of the terrine dish. Cut the polystyrene to shape and size and wrap tightly in cling film. Do the cutting outside as it is a bit messy. This doesn't work in the oven (I tried it!) so is only useful for use in cold terrines, but it allows you to make a smaller terrine in a large dish.

Paint brush
I buy mine from DIY stores. Do purchase them with 'no loss' bristles made of plastic.

Piping bag
Piping is a tricky skill to master. Only half fill and use one hand to guide at the bottom and one hand to squeeze from the top.

It is a neat way of adding ingredients to both terrines and verrines with precision.

Cream shipper or syphon
A stainless steel bottle which holds a pressure via a small gas charger. They are originally used for 'crème Chantilly' on top of desserts, ice cream and hot chocolate. These are very useful for light substances (see the foie gras recipe on page 157). You can now buy them from good cookware shops or the internet. Practice with different liquids and flavours – it's good fun!

Weights
I use a dumb bell weight to put pressure on the terrine but equally it could be a large tin of fruit or a jug filled with water. I would not use anything heavier than 3kg.

Sieve or Chinoise
I find a good sieve is an important piece of equipment in the kitchen. It is essential in producing a fine purée or mousseline.

Zester
Also called a grater. Use a stainless steel one which is very sharp, and I would always look for one with a flat handle as they are easier to hold and give the best results.

Index

Index

Index

Index

Terrine listing

Meat
Beef 'pot au feu' with green cabbage 27
Chicken, mozzarella & red onion compote 83
Cornfed chicken confit with mushrooms & baby leeks 29
Duck magret & quail breast confit cooked with apple 69
Ham & duck liver mousse with cherries & baby onions 67
Lemon chicken breast wrapped in pork belly slices 43
Rabbit & pheasant marinated in mustard 45
Spinach, ricotta & pancetta with grilled red peppers 85

Fish
Cooked crab with celeriac & baby squid 47
Lobster, crayfish & cod with red chard 49
Salmon, cod & prawn mousse with lemon & fennel 89
Seared tuna with avocado, new potatoes & coriander 25
Skate with gherkins, carrots & sushi nori 63
Smoked haddock mousse with herbs & cambozola 87
Smoked mackerel & trout with saffron potatoes 65
Smoked salmon & mozzarella with basil 23

Veg
Artichoke, asparagus, parsnips in beetroot jus 31
Caramelised onions, ham & reblochon cheese 91
Goats cheese, rocket & baby onions with chorizo 93
Old fashioned Macedoine presented as a mosaic 73
Sweet potato & celery with dill cream cheese 71
Three peppers & feta wrapped in grilled courgette 33
Two rice terrine with broccoli & cauliflower 51
Wild mushrooms & garlic with roasted turnip 53

Sweet
Coconut semolina with dried fruits 57
Dark chocolate & orange 55
Fresh citrus fruits with mint in an elderflower jelly 35
Frozen dried fruits & nuts in nougatine parfait 95
Mango & chocolate polenta 97
Mango & papaya with dates & raspberries 75
Pudding of figs, rhubarb, strawberries & blackberries 37
Vanilla Panacotta with cherries, plums & sultanas 77

Verrine listing

Meat
Aromatic crispy duck with pea salad 177
Bocconcini mozzarella, parma ham & parmesan 175
Diced pancetta with boursin & poached quails egg 111
Duck confit with marinated figs & fresh coriander 181
Foie gras cappuccino with quince jelly 157
Pig's trotters, roasted pak choi & pickled onions 135
Smoked chicken & cream cheese with asparagus 155
Smoked gammon with cranberries, apricots & nuts 113

Fish
Carpaccio of halibut with purple cress salad 171
Diver caught scallops with kipper, fennel & spinach 117
Fresh water prawns & cucumber mousse 153
Light grey mullet mousse with fresh cooked mussels 115
Mediterranean prawn salad with sesame dressing 173
Poached huss with beans & slow roasted tomatoes 131
Smoked salmon mousse with avocado guacamole 151
Tuna & marlin set in a light jelly with fresh salsa 133

Veg
Beetroot puree with a green bean salad 159
Cauliflower puree, creamy peas & black truffle flakes 121
Greek salad a la verrine 179
Ratatouille set in a Sauterne jelly, with tapanade 139
Red radish & mange-tout in watermelon jus 141
Sun dried tomato, goats cheese & rocket 161
Sweet potato & carrots with orange juice & cumin 119
Tagliatelle of vegetables set in orange dressing 137

Sweet
Apples in honey with fresh grapes & treacle top 123
Cherry, figs & raspberries in port & orange vinegar 183
Lemoncello & pistachio crème brulee 125
Orange & white chocolate bavarois with florentines 145
Pear poached in beetroot jus & roasted plums 185
Pineapple & strawberry with candied basil leaf 165
Thyme & lavender mousse with cherries 163
Trio of mango, chocolate & lemon custard 143

I dedicate this book to my two year old son Jack, being a Dad has given me the last push in my conviction to share and educate

I would never have realised this project without the help of my number one motivator - my devoted wife Judith. Her enthusiasm, energy and expertise fuel all my endeavours.

Thankyou also to my chefs, Kevin and Dave for their time and devotion.

John, my dad-in-law for his love, his encouragement and his endless sense of humour, he is always a welcome breath of fresh air.

To Ezra for believing in me, encouraging me and for being a 'no problem' kind of guy.

To Janet and Tony for listening, and for having the best place on earth to have a moan, thanks for you patience and advice.

Alain Cahour, the president of the Conseil Culinaire Francais of which I am a member, a good friend who is always there.

Thanks to Richard Faulks for his patience and pure natural talent to take such vibrant pictures. To Mik Baines, for his enthusiasm and hard work and for sharing his love and knowledge of all things to do with the motor vehicle. Thanks to Sam Street who crossed many bridges and faced many fears to help us and to Myra our silent partner who patiently checked my homework.

Thanks to Rupert for his support and for being the voice of reason behind this major commitment.

Thanks must go to Nick at the Golden Key in Snape, who accommodated us during a day's photo shoot and often more.

Thank you to Pillyvut our supplier of white china, and finally to Jan and Frank and the team at Accent Fresh our fruit & veg supplier who were behind us at the very beginning.

And a final and massive thanks to my panel of testers, to Janet, Esra, Sandra, Mary, Jane and Matt and to Gillian – your feedback was very much appreciated.

Merci!

Détendez! When the party's over and your guests have all gone, relax, take a well-earned rest then start planning your next kitchen adventure...

Terrines
&Verrines

Published by Food Creation Ltd
Halesworth, Suffolk, IP19 8QJ
info@foodcreation.co.uk
www.foodcreation.co.uk
www.franckpontais.co.uk

ISBN 13: 978-1-903872-09 3
First published in hardback
978 1903872093 2008

Print sourced by Navigator
info@navigatorguides.com
www.navigatorguides.com

Printed & bound in China by
C&C Offset Printing Co Ltd